Moral Education
in School

Moral
Education
in School

PHILIP R. MAY

 METHUEN EDUCATIONAL LTD
London · Toronto · Sydney · Wellington

First published 1971 by Methuen Educational Ltd
11 New Fetter Lane, London EC4
© *1971 by Philip R. May*

Printed in Great Britain
by Richard Clay (The Chaucer Press) Ltd
Bungay Suffolk

423 46290 3 Cased
423 46280 6 Paper

Distributed in the USA by Barnes & Noble Inc

Contents

v

Foreword

The moral development of children and young people has always been a matter which has provoked comment and concern. At the present time the subject of moral education is becoming increasingly prominent in educational discussions at all levels. There seems to be a growing body of opinion in favour of devoting more time and effort in the nation's schools to help pupils to achieve greater moral understanding and awareness. Partly for this reason a nationwide research survey was carried out by this author to discover more precisely what the teaching profession in general thought about moral education in school.

The purpose of this book is to examine the whole question of moral education in school. Many people would argue that for some time the main emphasis in our educational system has been on intellectual development, while moral and aesthetic education have rather been left to take care of themselves. A greater emphasis on children's moral development brings many problems. These will be considered along with such central issues as the teacher's role in moral education, and the basis of morality. It is in this setting that the results of the survey of teachers' attitudes are reported and analysed, with some details of a further research survey into adolescent attitudes to moral education in school. The final chapters raise some of the practical issues which have to be faced in the moral education of our children at school, and offer some suggestions as to what might be attempted, and possible teaching methods.

At the end of the book, Appendices detail some of the relevant research survey questions, and there is a brief index of names and other main references not indicated by the chapter headings.

Chapter 1

Education for Ichabod

Every year, several thousand students go from our university departments and colleges of education into full-time teaching posts. It is a fair assumption that the majority enter their profession a little nervous and uncertain perhaps, yet with enthusiasm and a real concern for their pupils, their subject and the work they are undertaking. There are no doubt some who regard teaching merely as one way to earn a living, or as something to do until marriage or a more lucrative post can be obtained. But most of the others firmly believe that the job they have chosen to do is exciting, rewarding and responsible, one which offers a real challenge and which is both satisfying and thoroughly worth while. And they are quite right. Yet after four or five years of teaching, what happens to that initial zeal? The care for pupils and subject is usually still there, but the enthusiasm is not so evident, particularly that confidence many of them once felt about the role and status of the teacher. Some of the early drive has been tempered by experience and youthful energies are being more wisely and effectively channelled. Yet the optimism of student days has largely disappeared.

It is hard to determine why this is so. It is not that the young teacher finds his older colleagues to be disillusioned and cynical, although sceptical attitudes are common in the profession to-day, often because many teachers feel that important decisions are out of their hands completely; too often there is a lack of proper consultation and this results in a feeling of helplessness and bitterness. Nor is it that after a time, teaching appears to lose some of its point. Despite the insistent demands of day-to-day involvement which take up most of a teacher's time and energy, most teachers never lose their sense of individual purpose. But there is a loss of wider vision. There is uncertainty and confusion both inside and outside the profession today about the role of the teacher at all levels. Care is choked and perspective is distorted too often by the complexity of the situation, by masses of detail in the daily round, by partisan selfishness and by a lack of assurance about the future. Absent from the speeches of our educational leaders at national level is that positive idealism, born of passionate and reasoned conviction, which provides both the framework for, and the basis of, policy and progress as well as high morale in education. The day of Ichabod has arrived. The glory has departed.

This is not to suggest that there are no ideals any more in educational discussion. Worthy slogans are still propounded. We are urged from time to time to educate for citizenship, educate for democracy, educate for life. And at all stages we are to 'educate the whole child'. What such phrases mean is difficult to judge, though they all have something about them which encourages assent. The major educational reports of the last few years from Crowther to Plowden also put forward aims and plans which received widespread condemnation. What these reports all proclaim, especially the Newsom report, is that people matter more than things. As a nation we profess to believe this. Most individual teachers do. But since what people *do* is the real clue to their truly held beliefs, it may well be that collectively we do not wholeheartedly believe this assertion. There does not seem to be much real stress *in practice* on personal relationships and the importance of every individual, despite much wonderful, daily work by many teachers. This apparent lack is closely linked to the problem of lack of vision in education today. Because education is concerned with persons, only those ideals which recognise the personal are likely to have the power to fire the imagination, and to determine the will. Yet despite all our protestations of sincerity, today we seem to be more concerned with the material than the personal.

Almost every week our national leaders tell us that our basic problems are economic. No one doubts the importance in the life of a country of a sound balance of payments and freedom from debt, yet the roots of national health go deeper than the successful management of the financial and commercial situation. It is true that economics play an ever growing part in the making of educational decisions in all spheres of teaching and learning. Inevitable though this may be, it is one of the obvious signs of that materialism which dominates educational thinking now. The various kinds of comprehensive schools and sixth form colleges, especially if purpose built, should have many advantages, but one wonders how far their claimed economic viability has proved to be the major attraction for many of their supporters. No one would deny that we want the best of everything for our children, but is it not significant that praise for the bright new schools too often stresses the buildings, equipment and grant allocations rather than improved personal relationships?

Another illustration of education's materialistic malaise is the high regard for qualifications in our society. They *are* important, and the more one has, the more opportunities become available. A recent advertisement had as headline: 'What your "A" levels will get you.' Is education becoming merely a means to 'getting and spending'? The race for 'O' and 'A' levels, diplomas and degrees is all-absorbing, despite the fact that these examinations can only test certain kinds of knowledge. There is so much

3

new knowledge, and it is essential in a modern technological society that most of our pupils should master this information, and, no doubt, be tested in it. But the resulting pressure can so often lead to the rejection by staff and pupils alike of activities and subject matter which are 'not in the syllabus'. The examinations cannot test the 'whole man', nor are they intended to. Yet for too many parents, employers and even some teachers now, education tends to be equated with so many examination passes. What is more, those equally sensitive, needy, worthy human beings who will never pass any of these tests are sometimes dismissed as 'dregs', 'duds', 'no-good'. Newsom drew attention to their needs. So to a lesser extent did Albemarle and Plowden. 'How right you are,' replied society, and continued largely to ignore them.

One further example of materialism in education must be mentioned. This is what Spencer Leeson once called 'the advancing tyranny of specialisation'. The root of the trouble is the fragmentation of the curriculum in most schools, especially at the secondary level. Many concerned with curriculum development are aware of this and are striving to overcome some of the attendant problems, especially those which inevitable specialist study creates. In his Bampton lectures, published in 1947 as *Christian Education*[1], Leeson argued that the increasingly narrow treatment of one's subject had grave dangers: 'Specialisation offers a way of escape from difficult and soul-searching issues.' It is safer and more comfortable to study one's subject in isolation, or to do minute research in one corner of the field. One gets so involved with one's subject that true purpose in education can become difficult to determine. And as Leeson noted, 'with purpose out of sight, there soon disappeared responsibility for everything wider than one's individual subject'. Here perhaps is where the greatest danger of specialisation lies. To stress this, however, is not to deny the value of study in depth for all who can benefit from it. Some specialisation in schools

4

is essential, particularly at the sixth-form level. Too strong an insistence on general education could lead to superficiality of learning. Yet an *over*-specialised or a 'Bitzer' curriculum provides no real vision or framework for the pupils, a framework of universal principles, values, aims, which give point to the whole educational process.

It is not that we have, like Eliot's chorus in *The Family Reunion*, 'lost our way in the dark'. But we have certainly lost our vision concerning the true end of education. We should reject all arguments which urge that the education of our children must be determined by economic expediency, administrative convenience and political whim, or by the demands of university studies, the individual's future job and the qualifications needed therein. They must not be ignored but they are not central. Education is basically a matter of relationships between teachers and pupils. It is a moral business. It is about the moulding and guiding of character and personality. The chief business of teachers is to help make men and women. Here we can learn much from the past. The great educators were great primarily because they had vision. Common to most of them was a vision of 'the good man'. Though they would not always agree with one another, they knew and in their various ways proclaimed that education was about people, not things. Perhaps our problems are greater today than theirs, because traditional standards, values and beliefs are much questioned, and often ignored even when lip service has been paid to them. We cannot take for granted, as Professor Peters in one place seems to suggest we can, such procedural principles as 'fairness, freedom, considering people's interests, and respect for persons'.[2] Nor should we, because they need re-examining and reproclaiming.

Sir Francis Bacon once wrote that 'prosperity doth best discover vice'.[3] We live in a prosperous country which enjoys a high standard of living. Whether our age is worse morally than previous times is debatable, and would be difficult to prove. Those who advocate individualistic ethical standards and greater permissiveness in moral behaviour often enjoy wide publicity to the dismay of those who hold orthodox and traditional viewpoints. Censorship of all kinds is under constant attack from certain quarters, and the demand for freedom to advocate or criticise as one pleases is insistent. These demands and attacks come in the main from a small but vocal minority, yet in an age when change is often equated with progress they seem to have growing influence. Certainly moral attitudes appear more tolerant than they were fifty years ago. We live in a closely knit society. It is therefore necessary that all members should have a real social concern for their neighbours. None the less, some observers of the social scene suggest that selfishness is more apparent in all walks of life today. Also the upsurge of violence is more frequent in society. How to tackle this kind of problem causes growing heart-searchings. Such factors as these may help to account for the anxiety now being expressed about the moral standards of the young.

Whether more concentration on the moral and spiritual development of our pupils will help us to recapture vision in education cannot be known unless we try it and see. As well as examination of the problems attendant on this task, such a demand also involves a thorough appraisal of the role of the teacher today. What follows in this book is an attempt to consider certain aspects of the position and function of the teacher in our maintained schools as regards children's moral development. The whole question of moral education in school will be scrutinised, and an analysis given of the views on this subject of the teaching profession itself. Their attitudes for and against the subject and their ideas and suggestions about it will be detailed. What they think on this matter is vital, since after the parents, the main responsibility for the moral development of our children is theirs.

REFERENCES

1. S. LEESON, *Christian Education*, Longmans, 1947.
2. R. S. PETERS, 'The Status of Social Principles and Objectives in a Changing Society', in *The Educational Implications of Social and Economic Change*, Schools Council Working Paper No. 12, H.M.S.O., 1967, p. 29.
3. FRANCIS BACON, 'Of Adversity', in *Essays*. It is part of the last sentence of that essay.

Chapter 2

The Demand for Moral Education

Schoolmastering has never been given in England the full respect and honour that is its due, and which the dominie has always enjoyed in Scotland. Attitudes to teaching have always varied greatly from country to country and at different times in world history. In ancient China teachers were second in general esteem only to the highest paid public servants, while only the high-caste Brahmin priests were the teachers in old India. Because of the importance of the teacher in Scripture, the Jews have always regarded teaching as a sacred office, in sharp contrast to Greek and Roman attitudes which often ignored the role of tutor to the very young, or assigned it to a slave or other menial. After the Reformation the great importance of the schoolmaster's task as a full-time job was emphasised by many in England and on the Continent who were followers of Luther and Calvin. It is worth adding that some of the most efficient practitioners at this time in Europe were to be found in Jesuit schools. In the eighteenth and early nineteenth centuries English schools were very inadequate indeed and only in the last fifty years or so has the position of teachers generally in this country improved so that understanding of the profession today is much more widespread and real.

8

Who then is to take up what a famous seventeenth-century schoolmaster once described as 'this despicable but comfortable employment of teaching School'?[1] The nature of the person who becomes a teacher is a matter of great importance and it is both interesting and revealing to consider how the character of the schoolmaster has been emphasised in the past, especially in the light of current discussions about moral education. Quintilian, the well-known Roman writer on education of the first century A.D., sets a very high standard. The master must have no vices himself nor tolerate any in his pupils. He must be friendly without being familiar, never lose his temper or ignore anything that merits correction, and be persevering and able to endure hard toil.[2] Erasmus desired teachers to be scholars of high character and attainment, men whose manner was gentle and sympathetic and who used wise and attractive methods of instruction. They should be able to sympathise naturally with their pupils and be ready to adapt themselves to the demands of youth.[3] In the seventeenth century Thomas Gataker, one of the great Puritan pastors, had the full-time schoolmaster in mind when he said: 'Teaching even of children is no base profession; it is that, that may well beseeme even the greatest',[4] and later in the century Richard Baxter frequently emphasised the need for 'clear-headed, well-studied, much-experienced godly men'.[5]

The statutes of particular schools especially indicate the main qualities looked for by those who were to appoint masters to teach. Those of Oundle in 1556 stressed 'That neither the Master nor Usher shall be common Gamesters, haunters of Taverns, neither to exceed in apparel, nor any other ways to be an infamy to the school, or give evil example to the scholars, to whom in all points they ought to show themselves examples of honest, continent and Godly behaviour.'[6] No one was to become 'master of the scholars' at Guisborough in North Yorkshire, 'except he be sufficiently learned and exercised in Grammar, honest in conditions and living, and a Priest in Orders at the time of his

B

admission, and no Scot or Stranger born'.[6] The Latin school-master at Chigwell in 1629 could have no doubts about what was required of him. He should be 'a graduate of one of the Universities, not under seven and twenty years of age, a man skilful in the Greek and Latin tongues, a good poet, of a sound religion, neither Papist nor Puritan, of a grave Behaviour, of a sober and honest conversation, no Tippler nor Haunter of Alehouses, no puffer of Tobacco; and above all that he be apt to teach and severe in his Government'.[6]

The emphasis throughout is on godliness and good learning. A study of advertisements for teachers and tutors in the eighteenth and nineteenth centuries reveals a similar stress on character and sense of vocation. For the schoolmaster was required primarily to be an inculcator of virtue. He was first of all a 'maker of good men'. Ability, learning, vocational skills were important but secondary.

What does society today wish its teachers to do in the schools? Current advertisements suggest that they are to be instructors in set tasks, skills and areas of knowledge. When parents visit the schools, discussions about particular pupils usually centre upon their intellectual development. Progress, or the lack of it, in academic subjects seems to receive more attention than anything else, especially at speech-day ceremonies when intellectual success is always extolled. Nevertheless such research as has been done on this matter indicates that both parents and teachers emphasise above all the two concerns which have always been underlined – sound learning and moral education.[7] Now more and more people concerned with the education of children and young people are openly stressing the importance of moral development. They are increasingly looking to the schools to play a more explicit part in the moral upbringing of their pupils.

Why is there this current public insistence on something with which teachers have always been expected to concern themselves? Several answers may be proposed and all have some validity. In the first place, there is always a need to introduce the young to the moral requirements of the society in which they live, and to inculcate acceptable standards of behaviour. We live in an age in which anti-authoritarian views tend to receive wide publicity. Whether our society is as permissive as our daily newspapers, for instance, sometimes suggest, is a matter for debate. Yet it seems there is no longer a generally accepted moral code, a set of standards about behaviour which everyone feels able to quote with confidence, whatever their own personal conduct may be. Long-acknowledged attitudes are being questioned with the result that many people are confused about moral standards. These facts in themselves may well cause the schools now to attempt less in the way of moral education. Alternatively, what help they continue to give may be much more tentative. It could be the case that many children and young people are neither being told what they ought to do nor helped to decide for themselves.

Widespread dissemination by the mass media of a great variety of opinions has increased the uncertainty about moral standards. There has also been a real decline in the influence of religion, and the authority of the Bible has been undermined for many. Consequently there now seems to be no clear framework of firmly based standards on which to lean. The Christian standards, even though they were often accepted unthinkingly, provided a security and an assurance which many people now lack. Another reason urging more specific moral education in school cites the rise in crime and violence, not least among young people, as evidence of the need for more moral instruction of children. Some of those who reject the authority of religion advocate more explicit moral education in school. They want young people through rational discussion to accept certain moral sanctions on personal, social and philosophic grounds. Others are showing a more conscious interest in moral education because they are dissatisfied with the materialistic pressures in education and society referred to in the previous chapter. They believe that the schools will help redress the balance if they re-emphasise personal development, especially the moral and spiritual aspects of this.

Whatever the motives, there is no doubt that demands for more definite moral education in school will continue to be made. It is interesting to note, as later chapters will show, that a majority of the nation's teachers clearly sympathise with these requests. Broadly speaking, they are in favour of a systematic moral education in the maintained schools. Equally interesting is the fact that many older secondary school pupils in all types of school appear to want specific moral education lessons. In my as yet uncompleted research enquiry into the attitudes of 14–16-year-olds to moral education, out of well over 3600 pupils from a random sample of schools throughout the country, over 70% stated that they would like to have such periods on their timetables, while less than 15% were opposed to the idea. A fuller account of this research is given in chapter eleven.

 The whole subject of moral education in school constitutes a huge problem to which there are no easy solutions. Those who want the schools to help certainly assume that they not only can but should do something about it. Are we casting teachers in the role of guardians of the nation's morals? Is moral education teachable at all, or is morality caught rather than taught? If it can be timetabled as a subject, however it be named, is there a distinctive body of knowledge or skills that can be communicated? Or is the sum total of all that can be attempted in such lessons the 'pious mush and moral exhortations' predicted by one sceptical schoolmaster? As well as questions of what to teach, there are problems of how to teach such material as is available. And who is to be responsible for this teaching? All these questions are considered later in the book, not least from the viewpoint of a representative cross-section of the teaching profession.

Traditionally there have been two main ways in which the schools have tried to foster the moral development of their pupils. The first approach has been to give explicit moral instruction, not infrequently using catechetical methods and moral homilies to introduce and impress society's moral imperatives on the young. This teaching was often authoritarian in manner and was reinforced by strict control of pupil behaviour. The second way is by indirect, incidental teaching. In the last fifty years or so, such moral guidance as English schools have given, has usually been casual and oblique. Nevertheless, although the most powerful determinant of any child's moral outlook and behaviour is his home background, schools can influence the moral development of children. The daily experience of a school's atmosphere and ethos, its general rules, organisation and administration and its standards and values, professed and practised, has undoubted effect in developing attitudes. The beliefs and expectations of the head and the teaching staff about their work and their pupils are quickly communicated. The discipline and example exercised by staff and pupils alike, and the objectives – with attendant rewards and punishments – that are extolled and worked for, affect moral understanding and behaviour. In the teaching of all subjects, in games and sports, through positions of responsibility and indeed every aspect of pupil involvement in the running of the school, so moral awareness is fostered. Most of all, moral education takes place in the day-to-day personal relationships between staff and pupils and among the pupils themselves, in the classroom environment and in the school grounds, learning to work, play and live together.

Many concerned with education argue that if all this is so, then there is no real need to set aside special time for moral education. The schools are doing as much as they can be reasonably expected to do. This argument may have some force in a stable society where moral standards and values are both generally agreed and implicit in all that goes on. Yet the great weakness always of attempting to influence the moral development of children and young people only in indirect and incidental ways is that no one can be certain that all pupils are truly being helped. Too many may be left in a sort of moral vacuum, especially when there is uncertainty about codes of conduct. If special time is set aside, therefore, there should be a much greater opportunity for teachers to make a systematised and analysable contribution to the moral education of all their pupils.

A further crucial question has to be faced. If more explicit moral education is attempted by our schools – and to enable this to happen, the problem of finding time for such teaching has to be solved – what results can fairly be expected from the special lessons? Other nations which include moral instruction on their school timetables might help with an answer. In France it is hoped that pupils will learn self-discipline through the intellectual nature of their studies. Official sources state that 'la morale' is founded 'sur le respect de la vérité et de la dignité humaine'. French primary schools have 'l'instruction morale et civique' on their timetables, and this consists usually of 'un commentaire des incidents de la classe'. At the secondary level there has been no 'instruction morale et civique' since 1953, but the weekly time allowance for French has been increased so that moral instruction may be given through 'explication de texte'. The 1920 New Zealand Education Act requires moral instruction for all pupils up to 14 years of age. The Education Department provides syllabuses for the teaching of all subjects including this one, but stresses that these are suggested, not compulsory, programmes. The aim here is to promote moral understanding and growth.

If moral instruction lessons become a feature of school timetables, it would be wrong to judge their success by the number of considerate, self-disciplined and generally well-behaved young people who eventually leave our schools. Such an attitude is as mistaken and unfair as that occasionally expressed view which argues that the success of religious education lessons should be measured by the number of faithful converts produced. Yet, as attitudes of people in other countries also show, this is the expectation of many who advocate specific moral instruction in school. The U.S.A., and more particularly Japan, are the two most recent examples of nations which have put direct moral education into their school curricula not least because of widespread public concern about rising juvenile delinquency rates and the increasingly militant independence of young people, especially students. Such hopes are understandable, but go too far because they ask too much of the schools. They set up a goal which moral education lessons do not aim to achieve, even though they may well make a contribution towards it. Development to moral autonomy depends on much more than one or two hours per week of moral education. Such sessions do not aim to pressurise, to condition or to indoctrinate pupils to adopt certain attitudes and to behave in those ways which society deems to be socially acceptable. What can reasonably be expected of them is that pupils will gradually be helped to grow in moral awareness, to understand as far as they are able, the nature of moral judgments, and to recognise the importance of consistent, considerate behaviour. The children must be led to see that the choice whether to behave considerately or not is an important choice – one which, whichever way it goes, will have many and widespread effects on how they will live. Attendance at moral education lessons will not guarantee that our young people's decisions will always be right, reasonable and thoughtful for others. It can enable them at least to recognise their responsibilities to themselves and to their neighbours. Then the preconditions for autonomous moral attitudes and conduct will have been established. And if we can increase the moral understanding and sharpen the moral insight of more of our future citizens, perhaps we shall have created conditions which at least make possible a more morally responsible society.

One constant problem for anyone who takes part in discussions about morality or moral education is to know exactly what people mean by the various terms they use. Words like 'moral', 'morality', 'ethics', 'character', are not easily defined and they have overtones of meaning which vary, depending upon the context in which they are being used. It will therefore be helpful, in the light of what teachers have said and written about moral education in school, to conclude this chapter by rehearsing the main meanings of these words, and to illustrate briefly something of their use.

Of the various usages of the word 'moral' that are listed in the Oxford English Dictionary, three stand out. Firstly the word means 'relating to character or disposition'. In particular it relates to the distinction between right and wrong, as regards the nature of a person or something he does. Consequently moral sense is the ability to grasp the difference between right and wrong. Although the term itself carries no suggestion of approval or disapproval, in common use it frequently implies that one action or one opinion is good or better than another. Most people would agree that a person is acting in a moral way if his behaviour is freely determined by himself. The element of conscious choice must be present. Secondly, when used of persons, the meaning is 'morally good', or virtuous. Moral virtue refers to particular excellence of character or disposition. Thirdly the term means being concerned with good and evil and the rules of right conduct. Thus one speaks of a moral law or requirement.

From a questionnaire they sent to juvenile court magistrates, probation officers and youth leaders, the Eppels claimed that four main categories of the interpretation of the word 'moral' emerged, plus two broad standpoints. The four categories suggested were 1) predominantly sexual, 2) predominantly religious, 3) predominantly social/humanitarian and 4) predominantly rational/psychological. The two broad standpoints are described as firstly, that which stresses the positive elements of morality, for example duty, obligation, responsibility, and secondly that which stresses the negative elements of morality, for instance restraint, inhibition and conformity.[8] In a research survey among the nation's teachers, to be described in detail later in this book, this author found that the teachers when answering a questionnaire interpreted the word in three main ways, philosophical – concerned with ethics and moral judgment, social – concerned with relationships with others and the social virtues, and religious. In interviews with both respondents and non-respondents to the questionnaire, however, many teachers equated 'moral' with 'morals', and for this they meant primarily sexual morality. Therefore their replies can be categorised in much the same way as those received by the Eppels, although in a different order of priority.

The term 'morality' also has three main meanings according to the Oxford Dictionary. First is the meaning: knowledge of moral science. Secondly it refers to moral qualities or endowments. Thirdly it means 'moral discourse or instruction, a moral exhortation'. The most common meaning of the term in popular usage is: acting in accordance with the accepted standards of society. Immorality is acting against these standards, especially in sexual behaviour. John Wilson says that 'morality is about what we ought to desire for its own sake, and not essentially about what we ought to do in order to achieve what we desire'.[9] A little earlier in his book he had commented that 'the notion of morality, as it affects moral education, includes much more than adherence to particular *mores*. It includes the notion of relating to other people as equals, and knowing what their interests are, as well as acting in accordance with those interests. Also . . . the notion of managing one's own desires and feelings in the right way, even if the interest of others is not involved.'[10] He and his colleagues have attempted to describe morality in terms of a number of moral components.[11] These are PHIL – the degree to which one can identify with other people; EMP – insight into one's own and other people's feelings; GIG – the mastery of adequate factual knowledge; DIK – the rational formulation of principles concerning other people's interests; PHRON – the rational formulation of principles concerning one's own interests; and KRAT – the ability to translate these principles into action; in a word, willpower. They admit that this scheme is vague and logically shaky, but it forms a helpful basis for discussion about what constitutes morality. Professor M. V. C. Jeffreys gives a definition of morality which includes what most people have in mind when they use the term. He says that morality is 'behaviour in accordance with certain standards of what is good and what is evil – striving for the good and rejecting the evil'.[12]

For some people, moral education can be equated with the study of ethics. Ethics is the science of morals. It refers to the manner of life of people and to their conduct. The Oxford Dictionary further says that it is 'the science of human duty in its widest extent, including besides ethics proper, the science of law, whether civil, political or international'.

The literal meaning of 'character' according to the dictionary is, 'a distinctive mark; a brand, stamp'. This meaning carries over into the figurative applications of the term, where it has several uses. It can refer to the particular essence of something, that which distinguishes something from everything else. It also means 'mental or moral constitution'. Usually the word is used with the implication of worth or goodness behind it. Thus 'a person of character' means one who is upright, trustworthy, a man of integrity. The phrase can also mean one who has particular idiosyncrasies which make him stand out from his fellows. The phrase 'a character reference' means a detailed report of a person's nature and qualities. When people ask teachers to concern themselves with their pupils' character development, they usually have in mind two main meanings. They want the teachers to bring out the positive, distinctive qualities which make each child an individual person, and they also want their children to become good, honest, reliable people. The teachers must set standards of moral excellence at which the children should aim. They must also concern themselves with the nature and needs of each individual pupil. R. S. Peters argues that if character training means efforts to ensure reliability of response in accordance with a code, then 'this would essentially be rather a limited sort of operation. It would not suggest any endeavour to get the trainees to understand the "reason why" of things. When, on the other hand, we speak of "moral education" we immediately envisage tackling people's beliefs; we think of questions of fact and questions of justification in relation to such beliefs.'[13] Peter McPhail, however, would go further than this and say that moral education is also concerned with improving people's behaviour.[14]

Lastly there is the phrase 'moral education', a blanket term which is not easily defined. Peters' words just quoted refer to one important aspect. The three main meanings of the term 'moral' are relevant, as is the whole question of character development. The phrase includes both direct and indirect moral teaching. So it in fact refers to the whole process of growth in moral awareness, moral understanding and distinctive moral action, a process which should culminate in rational, responsible thought and behaviour.

Whether more and more pupils *will* think and act more responsibly as they grow to adulthood is an issue which goes beyond the definable limits of moral education. Many people would say that this is ultimately a religious matter (using that term in its widest sense), because it raises the fundamental question of authority behind moral rules. 'Why should I be good, fair, considerate?' is a question most young people will legitimately ask. The answer that John Wilson appears to give – because it is the reasonable course to take – is not very satisfying, perhaps because such a reply does not provide much motivating force. The Schools Council moral education curriculum development researchers stress the more pragmatic answer – that it is more beneficial to all concerned and promotes better relationships. Here again, some people might reasonably argue that terms like 'beneficial' and 'better' also raise religious issues concerned with the true basis of morality. At the practical classroom level, it is at points like these that those who take the religious and moral education lessons could very profitably work together.

In the end, what matters most to a nation's well-being is its spiritual and moral health. Everything else for which it strives depends on this. Our nation even more today requires teachers of character who possess a real sense of vocation. We still want all of them to assist in the task of 'making good men and women'. If moral education lessons become a regular feature of school life, they could, properly used, increase the effectiveness of the schools' contribution to the moral development of our children.

REFERENCES

1. CHARLES HOOLE, *A New Discovery of the Old Art of Teaching School*, London, 1660, ed. E. T. Campagnac, Liverpool, 1913, p. iii.
2. Quintilian, *Institutio Oratoria*, Book II, Chapter 2.
3. Erasmus, *De Pueris Instituendis*, in W. H. WOODWARD, *Desiderius Erasmus concerning the Aim and Method of Education*, C.U.P., 1904, pp. 182–203.
4. T. GATAKER, *Certaine Sermons . . .*, London, 1637.

5. See P. R. MAY, 'Richard Baxter on Education', *British Journal of Educational Studies*, Vol. XV, No. 1, February 1967, pp. 60–73.

6. Quoted in FOSTER WATSON, *The English Grammar Schools to 1660*, C.U.P., 1908, pp. 127–131.

7. See, for instance, F. MUSGROVE and P. H. TAYLOR, 'Teachers' and Parents' Conception of the Teacher's Role', *British Journal of Educational Psychology*, Vol. XXXV, June 1965, Part 2, pp. 171–178.

8. E. M. and M. EPPEL, *Adolescents and Morality*, Routledge & Kegan Paul, 1966, pp. 34–35.

9. JOHN WILSON *et al.*, *Introduction to Moral Education*, Penguin Books, 1967, p. 65.

10. Ibid., p. 61.

11. Ibid., pp. 192–197.

12. M. V. C. JEFFREYS, *Religion and Morality*, Religious Education Press, 1968, p. 11.

13. R. S. PETERS, *Ethics and Education*, Allen and Unwin, 1966, p. 34.

14. *P.* MCPHAIL, 'The Motivation for Moral Behaviour', *Moral Education*, Pergamon Press, Vol. 2, No. 2, June 1970, pp. 99–106.

Chapter 3

Moral Development and Moral Education

Writers on education from ancient Hebrew and Greek times to the present day have acknowledged the paramount importance of the moral education of children. Despite this common agreement, and the manifest fact that the role of moral educator is central to every teacher's task, direct training in moral understanding and in the exercise of moral judgments is still rarely undertaken in the nation's schools as a deliberate, conscious policy. This is especially true of the education of the ablest pupils. Perhaps parents and teachers have hoped that the tone, atmosphere and values of each school would indirectly but effectively stimulate such growth in moral awareness as might be necessary for the children and young people in their care. At the time of the 1944 Education Act many people understandably but mistakenly looked to the religious education clauses of the Act to ensure that the nation's pupils would be made morally upright. Biblical studies have always been central to any religious knowledge syllabus. The constant Scriptural emphasis on righteous conduct would surely be instrumental in producing better people. Unfortunately it was and is erroneous and unfair to saddle religious knowledge teaching with such an aim. There are perfectly sound educational reasons to justify religious education lessons on all school timetables, but the moral motive is not one of these. It seems that more and more people are realising this. Such a recognition of the proper aims of religious education is yet another reason for the growing demand for more specific moral education in our schools.

A much more powerful reason arises from the growing understanding we now have concerning the moral development of children. Although research in this field has been, in England especially, limited and unco-ordinated, much more attention is now being paid by philosophers and psychologists to this aspect of children's growth. Furthermore, our knowledge of this most complex aspect of our individual make-up has reached a point where certain hypotheses may now be accepted as reasonably proved. Chief of these is the Piagetian theory that moral growth consists of development through a number of definite stages, and it may be useful at this point to give a brief though over-simplified account of this theory, and the main modifications to it that other research findings have proposed.

In 1932 the Swiss psychologist Jean Piaget published his seminal work on *The Moral Judgment of the Child*. In this he argued that the road to moral maturity is marked out by certain periods, which he associated with particular age groups. Every child has to pass through these set stages as he develops moral awareness and judgment, although not all children in fact do so. Of the three stages of most interest perhaps to the teacher the first is the egocentric stage, in which the child is really interested only in himself and his own concerns and is indifferent to the concerns of his peers. Piaget suggested that this period lasts roughly from 2 to 5 years of age. The next stage, covering the following five years or so of a child's life, sees the child becoming increasingly aware of and interested in others. Real playing together is experienced now. Rules are still regarded as absolute, coming from outside (and usually adult) authority, and they are accepted as such. Moral judgment is

23

usually founded upon the immediate, material consequences which are likely to result from actions taken, particularly when the individual is tempted to break rules and to do wrong. Punishment is considered to be the inevitable, to be expected result of misdemeanour, but at this period of development, it is vital that it be deemed to be fair. In other words, all wrongdoers should be dealt with in similar ways, and these ways should be justly related to the degree of seriousness of the offence committed. 'Moral realism' is the phrase Piaget uses to describe this kind of morality. By it he means the unquestioning acceptance of rules and their claims on conduct. He describes the moral constraint of adults upon children as 'a constraint which leads to heteronomy and consequently to moral realism'.[1] This heteronomous morality, when the child is subjected to the guidance and rule of adults and others in authority, is objective, not subjective.

The third stage in moral development is, to use Piaget's words, marked by 'co-operation which leads to autonomy'.[2] In the child's awareness of others there is now concern for their welfare and interests along with respect for them as persons. Moral judgments are not now based solely upon the authoritarian demands of law. The approach is much more subjective, and assessment will take into account intentions, motives and the particular situation demanding a moral judgment. Between the period of heteronomous morality and that of autonomous, rational morality, Piaget points out that there 'can be discerned a phase during which rules and commands are interiorised and generalised'.[3] Laws governing moral conduct have been accepted rationally and made a part of an individual's general outlook. Thus his judgments stem from his own personal inner code, and are not mere repetitions of an objective set of rules. The individual is now thinking and acting in a fully responsible way.

Subsequent research, some of it highly critical of Piaget, has in general confirmed the Piagetian theory of development

24

through several stages. There are no absolute boundaries separating these stages, nor is there any suggestion that every child will pass through every stage, leaving earlier attitudes behind for ever when a further stage is reached. Moral development proceeds along with a person's general development, and cannot be completely isolated from his intellectual, emotional and spiritual development. It is closely, though not absolutely, linked with intellectual development, being heavily dependent on one's ability to think and reason. As Piaget and others have shown, intellectual development is also marked by particular stages. The three which are in some measure similar to the stages of moral development already described, are the stage of pre-operational or pre-logical thinking, the stage of concrete thinking and the stage of abstract thinking. Only in the last of these is one able to handle concepts properly – to generalise, form hypotheses and think in abstract terms. Again age boundaries are flexible. Moral principles differ from other kinds of principle, most clearly in their rational nature. Undoubtedly, as research has shown, moral behaviour is influenced by a person's ability or lack of ability to reason. Some understanding of the stages of intellectual development, therefore, helps our understanding of moral development, and both are relevant to the subject of moral education.

Yet the cognitive is not the only constituent of morality. People often act in ways not determined by reason even when they accept the logical validity of a particular rational course that has been proposed to them. The influence of particular moral attitudes that they happen to hold is pertinent here. Various attitudes – rational, altruistic, personal, etc. – form during childhood, become established and help to determine an individual's response to particular people, objects or situations. This fact offers some explanation for the complex nature of moral awareness and moral judgment. It helps to account for the persistence in the morally mature person of judgments and

c

behaviour associated with an earlier form of morality.

The main modifications and refinements of Piaget's original findings, which other researchers have suggested, can be summed up in three groups. Firstly, different studies have shown that cultural and sub-cultural factors influence moral development. Perhaps the best known of these studies was the work of Lerner,[4] published in 1937. He discovered that with children of the same age and intelligence, distinctive differences in their replies were still noticeable, those from homes enjoying higher socio-economic status showing greater moral maturity than their less fortunate fellows. Havighurst and Taba in 1949[5] also noted class differences, while Peck and Havighurst have suggested that the influence of particular sub-cultures affects moral judgment and behaviour.[6] The most recent research in this area of the field has been done by John and Elizabeth Newson.[7] Undoubtedly the most significant influence on any child's moral development is that of his parents and home background.

Secondly, moral judgment and conduct are also influenced by various sanctions. McKnight[8] and Swainson[9] are two researchers who have interested themselves in this aspect of moral development, although unfortunately neither of their theses has been published. Briefly, it has been demonstrated that moral actions can be governed by prudential, authoritarian, personal and social principles. Religious sanctions and the claims of conscience should be added to this list. Finally, individual differences also influence moral development. Several researchers, notably Havighurst and Taba,[5] have considered the effect of an individual's personality structure upon his moral outlook and conduct. It can be concluded from their work that different personality types illustrate the various stages of moral development, and are closely linked to different moral sanctions. In other words, the way we behave depends very much on what sort of people we are.

Before leaving the subject of moral development, reference

must be made to the proposals of Kohlberg in America and Norman Williams of the Farmington Trust moral education research team. Kohlberg[10] has suggested six stages for moral development, grouped in three pairs. There is the pre-moral level when the child obeys to escape punishment or to gain rewards. Then comes the level of conventional role-conformity in which the child obeys to escape disapproval, reproof or blame and the shame which might follow such criticism. Thirdly comes the level of self-accepted moral principles. The two stages at this level are that of morality of contract in which the rights of others are respected and, if possible, never abused, and that of the morality of personal principles which the individual tries to keep to escape the censure of his own conscience. Kohlberg concludes that moral development is not simply the 'internalisation of external cultural rules, through verbal teaching, punishment or identification'. He claims that his evidence 'suggests the existence of a series of internally patterned or organised transformations of social concepts and attitudes, transformations which constitute a developmental process'.[11]

With a specific research project in mind, Norman Williams has also suggested that there may well be six stages of morality. These are 'a) morality based on obedience to external constraints, b) morality based on irrational introjected values, c) group-oriented morality, d) empathic morality, e) morality based on the ego-ideal, and f) rational morality'.[12] In Williams' research programme nearly 800 children aged from 4 to 18 in schools in various parts of the country were interviewed. Their responses to questions on seven areas of moral thinking – their ideas of good, ought, bad or naughty, fair, stealing, lying and bullying – were grouped into 17 distinct categories. Fourteen of these, all implying some form of behaviour control, were then classified into four groups, expedient (self-considering) responses and responses revealing irrational inhibition (self-obeying), both of which sets of replies he describes as 'self-related', and empathic responses (concerned with other people's feelings and needs) and authoritarian (other-obeying) responses, both of which groups Williams delineates as 'other-related'.

Significantly, Williams found a great variety of responses from all the children interviewed, even the four-year-olds. His proposed scheme has much in common with that of Peck and Havighurst, but his findings seriously question some of the assumptions of those who favour the developmental approach. If such an approach is valid, one would expect the responses of a particular child or age-group to be more in one category than the rest. Williams did not find any evidence of this. The 'developmentalists' have never really proved that the stages of moral growth that they propose are in fact consecutive, perhaps because they fit in so well with the Piagetian stages of cognitive development. Williams' evidence also largely appears to fit in with these cognitive stages, but it denies the theory of chronological development. He seems to argue that moral growth is cumulative, and he suggests three stages in a process of development towards generalisation of moral response. There is 'the stage of specificity' in which the child approaches each situation separately. Then there is 'the stage of overlap or partial generalisation' when the possibility of conflict between modes of moral thinking appears. Lastly there is 'the stage of stability' in which, when conflict arises, the individual has established for himself his own order of preference among the modes of moral thinking, and generalises accordingly. In his published work Williams has not yet clearly shown whether or not he really supports or disapproves of the notion of stages of moral development. The framework he has posited contains a hierarchy of moral responses. Presumably development should be encouraged from the lesser to the greater, the lower to the higher, the naïve to the mature. Answers to these and other queries will doubtless be given when his research programme is completed.

The deeper understanding of children's moral development

that all this research provides for us, has a significant contribution to make to the discussion concerning moral education in our schools. Of all the arguments in support of much more consciously planned moral teaching, two stand out. The first is psychological, and draws upon the evidence of growth in moral development and modes of moral thinking. Teachers need to be aware of the different modes and stages so that they may organise their teaching methods to suit as far as possible the particular level which their pupils may have reached. Pupils in any particular class may well be at different stages of moral awareness, although in his general instruction the teacher usually has to assume that a majority of the class are at roughly the same level. If the ethos and atmosphere of the school likewise take account of these stages, our children may well make more rapid and positive progress in moral development. R. S. Peters makes the point that 'teachers must have a good grasp not only of the stages of moral development but also an insight into the position of individual children in relation to such stages. But behind all such understanding there is the question of respect for persons which is very much at stake when matters to do with extenuating circumstances and the age of responsibility are under discussion.'[13]

The second argument approaches the discussion from the philosophical point of view. All human beings possess a sense of right and wrong. This sense seems to be an intrinsic part of human nature. It is largely, though not in all respects, analogous to the direct perception of the external world by the senses, and has something in common with the rational perception of truth and the consciousness of personal identity. Moral perception and judgment are an essential aspect of what we mean by being truly human. Moral consciousness is a unique and peculiar type of human experience. Moral judgments, although depending on intelligence, social status, personality and on the age and experience of each individual person, are distinctive.

29

They resist all attempts to reduce them to some other form or forms of discourse. The feeling of being 'bound' to do something, the obligation to approve certain motives or actions, the consciousness of liability and responsibility implied in the use of the word 'ought', these form a logically self-contained area of discourse which is *sui generis*.

It seems therefore that one mode of intellectual activity, one particular way of looking at the world, is the moral one. This approach parallels other approaches such as the logical, scientific, historical, religious and aesthetic. One category of human experience is the moral, and it is associated with a particular set of concepts. Consequently, the same argument that may be reasonably used to justify the existence on school timetables of such subjects as mathematics, science, history and religious knowledge is also relevant to support those aspects of moral education which may be organised on subject activity lines. We need to initiate children into this main aspect of human experience in addition to the others.

Our children and young people must be taught both to understand and how to apply moral concepts, and to see the significance of behaving or not behaving in a consistent way that recognises the needs and interests of others. A clear framework of rules is essential to their moral growth, although enforced learning of and obedience to such a code is not the end of moral education. Children should be helped to develop through the various stages, and in fact to take each step forward themselves, if they are to achieve autonomous morality, when they act responsibly, consciously, rationally on *their own* moral principles. This is not to suggest that they will have necessarily overthrown the set of moral laws which assisted their development during childhood. Nor is a situation envisaged in which each autonomous individual has a personally worked out code which may well clash with that of most other persons. It is argued elsewhere that certain moral rules are absolute and can

30

apply to all men at all times, everywhere. There is no contradiction between the existence of moral rules that are absolute and a person's autonomous acceptance of them for himself. The main aim of moral education is to encourage every child to develop as fully as possible in moral understanding and judgment. The hope is that the great majority will become responsible, mature, morally autonomous members of the community.[14]

REFERENCES

1. J. PIAGET, *The Moral Judgment of the Child*, Routledge & Kegan Paul, 1932, p. 193.

2. Ibid.

3. Ibid.

4. E. LERNER, *Constraint Areas and Moral Judgment in Children*, Wisconsin, U.S.A., 1937. See also his article, 'Perspectives in Moral Reasoning', in the *American Journal of Sociology*, Vol. 63, 1937, pp. 249–269.

5. R. J. HAVIGHURST and H. TABA, *Adolescent Character and Personality*, John Wiley, 1949.

6. R. F. PECK and R. J. HAVIGHURST, *The Psychology of Character Development*, John Wiley, 1960.

7. J. and E. NEWSON, *Patterns of Infant Care in an Urban Community*, Penguin Books, 1965. See also their section: 'Some social differences in the process of child rearing', in *Penguin Survey of the Social Sciences*, Penguin Books, 1967.

8. R. K. MCKNIGHT, *The Moral Sanctions of the Child*, Unpublished B.Ed. thesis, Glasgow, 1950.

9. B. M. SWAINSON, *The Development of Moral Ideas in Children and Adolescents*, Unpublished D.Phil. thesis, Oxford, 1949.

10. L. KOHLBERG, 'The Development of Children's Orientations Towards a Moral Order', *Vita Humana*, Vol. 6, 1963,

pp. 11–33, especially pp. 13–14. (Some readers will find it more convenient to consult N. Williams' summary of Kohlberg's findings in J. WILSON *et al.*, *Introduction to Moral Education*, Penguin Books, 1967.)

11. Ibid., p. 32.

12. Quoted from D. GRAHAM, 'Children's Moral Development', in H. J. BUTCHER (ed.), *Educational Research in Britain*, U.L.P., 1968, pp. 101–118. The quotation comes from p. 114 of this most useful and succinct account of research in this field. See also N. WILLIAMS' two articles on Children's Moral Thought, in *Moral Education*, Vol. 1, No. 1, pp. 3–12, and Vol. 1, No. 2, pp. 1–6, Pergamon Press, 1969.

13. R. S. PETERS, *Ethics and Education*, Allen and Unwin, 1966, p. 289.

14. Since this chapter was written, a comprehensive account of the moral development of children has been published, with detailed summaries of relevant research. The interested reader is commended to consult A. W. KAY, *Moral Development*, Allen and Unwin, 1968.

Chapter 4

The Teacher's Role in Moral Education

In a chapter on the aims of primary education, the Plowden report[1] stresses the need 'to fit children for the society into which they will grow up' (para. 494). Children will need to be adaptable, to be capable of adjusting, to live with others with respect and understanding, to discriminate, to be well-balanced, capable of learning new skills and able to understand their obligations (para. 496). The all-round development – religious, moral, mental and physical – of the individual is emphasised along with the gaining of basic skills necessary in contemporary society. The importance of co-operation between home and school is underlined, and in paragraph 505 we are reminded that 'a school is not merely a teaching shop, it must transmit values and attitudes'. So much for the most recent report on the primary schools.

At the secondary level another Central Advisory Council report,[2] named after its chairman Sir John Newsom, also offered a variety of suggestions in its chapter on 'Objectives'. 'Skills, qualities of character, knowledge, physical well-being, are all to be desired', along with 'capacities for thought, judgment, enjoyment, curiosity'. The pupils 'need to develop a sense of responsibility for their work and towards other people, and

33

to begin to arrive at some code of moral and social behaviour which is self-imposed'. They should also 'have some understanding of the physical world and of the human society in which they are growing up' (para. 27). They 'need to achieve some compassionate insight' into major world problems, they should be helped to make effective use of their leisure time, be given some training in discrimination, and be encouraged to think about issues of conduct and religion (para. 28). Later (para. 205), the report urges that 'positive guidance to boys and girls on sexual morals is essential'.

This report was concerned with pupils of average and less than average ability, in the 11–16 age group. A report on the ablest children in that same age range is not needed to stress the importance of high-level academic training for those capable of benefiting from it, as well as all the other aspects of education mentioned by Plowden and Newsom. It is quite obvious from these quotations that the task of the teachers at both the primary and secondary stages is a huge and complex one. The schools are not wholly responsible for the all-round education of the nation's children, but as these reports show, they are expected to play a major part. As for the teachers needed, only men and women of wide specialist knowledge, maturity and strength of character and considerable technical ability can be expected adequately to undertake the necessary duties with some hopes of success.

The problem of the role of the teacher today is very complicated. Whatever school he may be in, he has a number of functions to perform and in fact several roles to play. That these roles can and do conflict only makes his task more difficult. For instance, to satisfy certain of the demands of academic study *may* mean that the teacher must restrict the time spent on activities which more readily assist character development. It is never easy to decide where to strike a proper balance. Even within one specific role there are difficulties. Should the teacher of English, for example, refuse to enter his class of sixteen-year-olds for the 'O' level literature examination, study for which, he believes, demands much unprofitable slog at a very restricted syllabus? They are not mature enough to tackle the kind of literary study which such an examination requires, he argues. He wants to teach them a much more varied series of books, to help them to enjoy literature. Yet to deny certain pupils the chance to take the examination in English literature may well deprive them of the one extra subject pass they need to qualify for a particular job or to go on to further study. What is he then to do?

More broadly, all teachers have both an educational and a social role. Within the school they are teachers of subjects, imparters of the cultural heritage, inculcators of academic standards. They want to convey and develop a real interest and delight in the various aspects of the curriculum and through these, a deeper awareness of the world outside the classroom. They hope to encourage certain attitudes to learning and they set standards which make demands on their pupils. Children need to recognise and accept for themselves 'the best that is known and thought in the world'. R. S. Peters sums it all up by stating that 'the overall aim of education is to get children *on the inside of*' (– another favourite phrase of his is 'to initiate them into' –) 'the activities and forms of awareness characterising what we would call a civilised form of life'.[3]

But their orientation is not only in relation to the school. The teacher's task is also related to the life of the whole community. The social role has traditionally been expressed in such phrases as 'education for citizenship' and 'education for life'. At the most elementary level this has meant helping children to learn acceptable manners and the basic social graces. The teacher of infants in particular has to spend much time assisting her pupils in dress, eating habits, washing and toilet training. All schools have a concern for the health of their pupils and try to encourage in them, through the wise exercise of authority, habits of self-discipline, concern for others and a general sense of responsibility. Vocational training and guidance also come within this social role, as the work of counselling becomes more common in the schools. Some, like J. B. Mays for instance, are now urging a much wider social role upon teachers, especially those who work in slum, inner-urban and other culturally deprived areas. It is suggested that they should consider themselves as applied social scientists and, where necessary, take on the role of cultural missionaries.[4]

Because the main emphasis of this book is upon moral education in school, a full analysis of the role of the teacher will not be given here. It is important, however, to establish clearly that all teachers at every level are involved in moral education. Whether they like this or not, their daily duties unavoidably implicate them in the moral upbringing of their pupils. The tasks of the teacher in loco parentis demonstrate this fact.

THE TEACHER IN LOCO PARENTIS

Nothing has been said in statutory law about the teacher being in loco parentis, although the parental responsibilities of teachers have frequently been subsumed in case law. If he is to contribute effectively to the full development of his pupils, then the teacher must at least be assisting parents in carrying out some of their duties. In a complex and highly specialised society such as ours, parents are in fact delegating to the schools some of their authority and some of the tasks for which they still bear the prime responsibility. No parent, no matter how well educated and enlightened, can hope to provide all the knowledge and skills that children need in a technological age. Nor can he usually give the vocational training and careers guidance required. In the supervision of meals and play, in religious and moral education, in the teaching of hygiene and sex ethics, the teacher now shares duties that were once regarded as the special province of the home. The same is true of many extra-curricular and leisure-time activities in which teachers take a prominent part.

Again, in the much less easily definable area of personal relationships, teachers at all levels frequently find themselves in 'parental' situations. Although no other person can replace the love of the parents for their children, all teachers must have a real care and concern for their pupils. For as the Puritan Thomas Gataker rightly said, 'where no love is, there is little hope of learning'.[5] Also in the exercise of discipline the teacher acts in loco parentis and not merely as a responsible adult or agent of society. Many teacher–pupil relationships have close analogies with the relations between parents and children. This is particularly true of all primary school and class and form teachers. Chances for informal contact vary tremendously from school to school and even from teacher to teacher, but they form part of a teacher's parental role. The role differs according to the type of child being taught, the school one is in and the type of person one is as a teacher. Probably the teacher in the maintained school system is more in loco parentis with younger children than with middle- and upper-school pupils in secondary schools. But the role for most teachers is an imprecise one. The teacher is not a super-parent. Nor does he take the place of *any* kind of parent. The term 'in loco parentis' presumably has in mind 'the wise and reasonable parent' of the lawyers, the good, sound, average parent approved by society as a whole. It would be difficult to argue that this role excludes concern with children's moral education.

Of all the adult members of a school community, the head most clearly acts in loco parentis in almost all that he does. The final responsibility for all that takes place in his school is his. He has, in law, certain well-defined duties to perform, and in some of these he plays a role which is equally in loco parentis.

37

Firstly he has a responsibility, under the 1944 Education Act, to ensure that a daily act of school worship takes place. Secondly, he is usually responsible, at the secondary level particularly, for the choice of his staff, his wishes normally deciding the appointments. Being ultimately responsible for what is taught in his school, he has a duty to all concerned to ensure that in all aspects of his school's curriculum, what is taught is wholesome and sound. In the third place, the discipline of a school depends finally on the headteacher. In this respect (to oversimplify in order to make the point) he represents both law and love, both the state and the home. Again, he must ensure the effective administration and welfare of the school community. He is truly in loco parentis here, being immersed every day in a thousand details concerned with the running of his school, and the lives of his pupils. Lastly, the head in most schools has much responsibility for the giving of advice and guidance about the progress and future of his pupils. He has to tackle an increasing number of personal problems which confront his pupils – moral problems of all kinds, problems of individual personalities and of personal relationships, leisure-time problems and so on. Therefore no head can avoid exercising an authority and care akin to that of the parent.

How any teacher is to act in loco parentis with and for any child will be determined mainly by particular circumstances relevant to each individual case. In practice therefore his 'parental' activities vary widely according to the nature and needs of the child, its home background, age and ability, the type of school concerned and his own position therein. In general, it is reasonable to say that at all times when parents entrust their children to the care of the schools, then the teachers have a 'parental' role to play.

It follows from all this that if the teacher is to fulfil his responsibilities 'in loco parentis', let alone the educational objectives listed for him in the Plowden and Newsom reports, he cannot avoid being actively concerned in the moral education of his pupils. Character development, relationships with others, conduct and discipline, religious teaching, all are central issues in this part of any child's upbringing. The 1944 Education Act states that 'it shall be the duty of the local education authority for every area, so far as their powers extend, to contribute towards the spiritual, moral, mental and physical development of the community by securing that efficient education throughout those stages shall be available to meet the needs of the population of their area'.[6] It can be argued that here is society's legal expression of the public mind, requiring teachers to be involved in moral education.

Parents want the schools to help their children to acquire acceptable standards of behaviour. Research has confirmed that the children themselves are keen to discuss moral questions, and they especially value guidance concerning what is right and wrong in many spheres.[7] On educational grounds alone it is essential to assist pupils to grow in moral awareness. Part of what is meant by being human is the understanding of obligations and duties, rights and the claims of conscience, the whole field of moral discourse which belongs only to homo sapiens. Erase the moral dimension from a person's consciousness and he becomes a beast. Moral awareness is thus a fundamental facet of human understanding. If schools are to educate 'the whole child', as teachers frequently say they should, they must not ignore any pupil's moral understanding. For questions of private and public behaviour and of social relationships, and the exercise of moral judgment, are matters of practical necessity for all children as for all adults, in their studies as well as in everyday living. Therefore every teacher has an inescapable responsibility concerning the moral education of all the pupils in his charge.

THE TEACHER AS MORAL EDUCATOR

Three areas stand out as the spheres in which he can try to influence and assist the moral development of the children in his care. The first of these is the subject or subjects he teaches, where he will both advocate and set certain definite standards. Every subject has its own criteria and values which, with the discipline of study, make intellectual and moral demands upon student and teacher. Success in the academic field at both elementary and advanced levels requires certain qualities – imagination, determination, persistence, objective judgment, patience, integrity and so on. Thus in the daily round of teaching and learning, children should be growing in moral awareness and experiencing enrichment of personality, through their studies. In all that takes place the teachers usually take care not to impose their own opinions arbitrarily upon their pupils. R. S. Peters states that 'in the sphere of attitude training, the teacher must accept the fact that he may be regarded as a traditional status-holder towards whom either total deference or defiance is due. He has to start from this attitude to himself and work gradually towards developing a more rational attitude towards an office which he happens to occupy.'⁸ This may also be said of the subject he teaches. Also teachers have to beware of encouraging the adoption of purely subjective attitudes and standards. An essential part of the 'discipline' of a subject lies in helping pupils to recognise and understand wider, more all-embracing views.

The second sphere of moral influence of the teacher concerns the way he encourages his pupils to behave towards himself, towards one another and to the whole community. Every school demands certain standards of behaviour from its pupils. Every teacher must also establish what he expects of the children he teaches, both in lessons and as they move about the school and its grounds. At different stages of their school life, children will be taught manners approved by the school community.

They will be expected to behave in an orderly and considerate way in all they do. Some of this teaching will reinforce that of the parents. Sometimes it will run counter to the child's experience at home and in the local environment. None the less, most parents expect the teachers to maintain clear standards of behaviour, wanting the schools to help their children to discriminate and 'to learn right from wrong' generally.

John Wilson affirms that the job of the teachers as moral educators is to bring up their pupils 'to be rational and to form their own values: to instil respect for, and capability at applying the second order principles relevant to morality' (he instances, for example, respect for persons and concern for other people's interests), 'and neither to produce conformity nor to encourage rebellion'.[9] They must, in short, be brought up to be 'free and rational adults'.[9] This implies, among other things, that the children will have contact with adequate models of free, rational adulthood. Herein lies the third sphere of moral influence in which teachers may help their pupils – that of personal example. It is an age-old truism that example usually exerts a more powerful influence than precept. Whether children see in their world of school, be it run as an extended family, as a democracy or as a benevolent autocracy, the most responsible, conscientious adults of their community is an interesting point. Nevertheless, even though as some researchers have shown, school leavers quickly reject some of the values they were taught at school as 'irrelevant to real life', and even though the ethos of home always exerts a more powerful influence than that of the school, in the area of inter-personal relations teachers undoubtedly affect their pupils by their own conduct and reactions to the day-to-day incidents of school life. How they respond to their pupils and colleagues is crucial. To have a really positive effect they should have developed, to use the language of Michael Argyle and others, an interactional style which is socially effective.

If the teacher is to do his work effectively, he must demand

D

conformity to certain rules, and encourage reasonable behaviour. This raises again the whole question of discipline. Discipline has at least a threefold purpose. Firstly it develops an awareness of law. Secondly it develops moral awareness in the individual, giving him a fuller understanding of himself and his own nature. Thirdly it helps a person to recognise his moral obligations to others for the smooth running and welfare of society as a whole. Thus in the exercise of discipline in the family and at school, parents and teachers not only wish to establish order for the benefit of all, but also hope to help their children to be *self*-disciplined. This is not a mere passive conformity to a set of rules imposed from above, but behaving in a rational, responsible manner by one's own free choice. The teacher's task is made more difficult by the current questioning of the basis on which his moral authority rests. In fact, it rests on both his office and his person. As a teacher he is a representative of authority and should be respected principally because of his office. The validity of his moral authority depends also upon his personal character and upon the personal relationships he manages to establish. And his success in the realm of moral education depends on the recognition and acceptance by his pupils of the fact that men everywhere are responsible for their actions.

All three areas of moral influence – the teaching of a subject, helping with behaviour and the teacher's personal example – cannot be separated in most of what a teacher does. Some would say that he has no distinct role as a moral educator. He takes this task upon himself when he becomes a teacher, and moral education is just another part of the business of teaching. It could be argued there is no such entity as moral education pure and simple. Nor is it merely a matter of finding the right answers, telling the pupils what these are and persuading them to act upon them. Perhaps the first task is to define a standard of behaviour for our particular place and time in history and for our particular generation, a code of conduct considered worthy and socially acceptable. Without clear and definite standards it it extremely difficult for a person to learn to choose responsibly, or to act or refrain from acting with a proper restraint. In educating their pupils with these standards in view, teachers should strive, as philosophers like R. S. Peters, P. H. Hirst and John Wilson strongly urge, to initiate their children into the relevant principles in such ways as will help them to act responsibly as far as possible through their own free, autonomous choice.

A second immediate task for teachers is to decide what they think constitutes 'good character' as regards their pupils. Children mostly have a keen sense of ethical awareness, and often demonstrate a high degree of moral knowledge, although possessing moral knowledge does not necessarily guarantee praiseworthy moral behaviour. Teachers should be clear about the sort of persons they hope to see their pupils become, and about the moral principles they wish young people to uphold. This requirement of all who educate the young will become more urgent as the demand grows for more moral education in the schools. For as Professor M. V. C. Jeffreys has pointed out, 'in the long history of nations, virtue matters even more than knowledge, values than information'.[10]

REFERENCES

1. *Children and Their Primary Schools*, (The Plowden Report), H.M.S.O., 1967.
2. *Half Our Future*, (The Newsom Report), H.M.S.O., 1963.
3. R. S. PETERS, *Ethics and Education*, Allen and Unwin, 1966, p. 81.
4. See, for instance, his *The School in its Social Setting*, Longmans, 1967.
5. THOMAS GATAKER, *Certaine Sermons*, London, 1637, p. 5.
6. 1944 Education Act, Ch. 31, Pt. II, 7.
7. See, for example, H. LOUKES, *New Ground in Christian Edu-*

cation, S.C.M. Press, 1965, and Schools Council Enquiry I, *Young School Leavers*, H.M.S.O., 1968.

8. R. S. PETERS, op. cit., p. 316.

9. J. WILSON *et al.*, *Introduction to Moral Education*, Penguin Books, 1968.

10. M. V. C. JEFFREYS, *Religion and Morality*, Religious Education Press, 1968, p. 41.

Chapter 5

Moral Education in School
– a Research Survey

In the last four or five years positive steps have been taken to examine the question of moral education in the country's maintained schools. The first of these to be widely publicised was a document entitled *Religious and Moral Education*, printed in October 1965, and containing some proposals for county schools by a group of Christians and Humanists.[1] This group felt that 'a more open approach is needed in religious education', and desired 'to give moral education a more definitely considered place in the work of the school'.[2] They were not recommending that there should be two alternative courses in school, one on religious education and the other on secular moral education. They did want more definite planning for moral education. Therefore they offered the suggestion that 'part of the education offered to all pupils should be explicitly planned to help them to prepare themselves for responsible living and, within the limits of their experience, to consider "the nature and destiny of man" '.[3]

The discussion of the issues they raise remains, probably by design, at a fairly general level. Hardly anything is offered as possible content for the courses in moral education, nor is the equally difficult problem of methods of teaching such

45

courses really considered. They tend to assume that syllabuses which command ready agreement could easily be devised. More is required of those who plan and execute such courses than acceptance of 'the principle of what is for Christians the second commandment: Thou shalt love thy neighbour as theyself'.[4] They recognise that the teachers who operate these courses may well need specific training, and they recommend that university departments of education, and colleges of education, provide help in this matter. Whether sufficient practising teachers can be found who can and will carry out effective moral education lessons is not seriously questioned. None the less, the pamphlet is stimulating, as well as sincere, and it has succeeded in its aim to start people talking openly about the proposals it makes.

A second even more significant step in the field of moral education was the setting up by the Farmington Trust, also in October 1965, of a special Research Unit in Oxford to conduct research on the topic of moral education. The director of this Unit is the philosopher John Wilson and he is assisted by two research fellows, the psychologist Norman Williams and the sociologist, Barry Sugarman. This project is expected to last for at least ten years, and the Unit has already published an important book, *Introduction to Moral Education*, to which all three researchers have contributed. The aim of this volume is to try to 'make sense of moral education as a *topic*',[5] and it is divided into three sections. The first, and by far the longest part, attempts to answer the question – 'What is moral education?'. Part II discusses the relevance of psychology and sociology to the subject, and in the brief final section practical suggestions are made on what to do about moral education. Discursively written, the book poses, and attempts some answers to, many relevant questions, and a basis is established for the Unit's subsequent research, some of which has already been referred to in chapter three of this book.

Thirdly, the Schools Council have also set up a major research project concerned with moral education, under the direction of Mr. Peter McPhail. This work, begun in September 1967 and again based at Oxford, is part of the Council's studies in curriculum development. The task of the Moral Education Curriculum Project is to design, test and develop curriculum material to help secondary school children find and adopt 'better' solutions to inter-personal problems. Included among the topics being investigated for their possible contribution to the moral education of children and young people, are school worship, the teaching of literature and school organisation, and the researchers hope to produce what they call 'sensitivity material', designed to increase young adolescents' awareness of the feelings of other people, and the degree to which they might take account of such feelings when making decisions affecting others. At the time of writing this chapter, much work has been done by the Project. It is now concerning itself with situational material (the situations having been provided by adolescents who regard them as important) covering the range of individual problems, interaction in the dyad, conflicts of interests between individuals and groups, and finally, the kind of organisations which facilitate the 'considerate style of life' – those, that is, which make it easier to take into consideration other people's needs, interests and feelings. A full report of this research is expected to be published in 1971.

Lastly, two practical projects by local education authorities are worthy of mention. These are the attempts by the county authorities of Gloucestershire and Wiltshire, the latter in fact following the scheme prepared by the former, to devise practical programmes on education for personal relationships. Syllabuses on this theme were worked out firstly for secondary school pupils in their first year, and then for pupils in the fourth, fifth and sixth forms. Details of these syllabuses and an account of the

47

aims and planning of the whole projects have been published in reports issued by the two authorities.[6]

Other local education authorities are also showing a growing interest in problems of moral education. Several of those who are undertaking the revision of their agreed syllabuses for religious education are paying particular attention to proposals to include suggestions related to moral education, and there may well be others who are preparing to follow the lead taken by Gloucestershire. Moreover, the subject is beginning to figure more prominently at teachers' conferences, and in teacher training courses. It is virtually certain, therefore, that the topic will increasingly engage the practical attention of the teaching profession.

What do the teachers themselves think about the subject of moral education? Are they in favour of the creation of special courses, however titled, for their pupils, courses which involve the setting aside of special periods each week or at certain times in the school year? What do they think should be included in the content of these lessons, and who should teach them? If they are against direct teaching on moral education in the nation's maintained schools, what are the reasons for their opposition? It was in order to try to discover answers to these and other related questions that in 1967 I set up a nationwide research survey into the attitudes of teachers to both moral and religious education. The remainder of this chapter will describe that survey and record its main findings concerning moral education in school.[7]

THE SAMPLE

420 maintained schools selected at random from education authority lists were approached and 337 (80%) agreed to help in the enquiry. Copies of the questionnaires used were then sent to these schools along with a letter explaining to each teacher

taking part the nature and purpose of the research. 311 schools, 92% of those to whom forms were sent, and 74% of all schools approached, actually replied. These schools were of all types, primary, secondary modern, secondary grammar, comprehensive and technical. They were situated in all kinds of areas – rural and mining towns and villages, larger towns and cities, urban middle class and inner urban industrial districts, new and old housing estates – in all parts of the country. They also varied considerably as regards the number of pupils in attendance. For purposes of comparison, schools in five local and county education authorities were chosen for particular attention. These were County Durham, Buckinghamshire and Berkshire, whose returns were combined, Leeds and Portsmouth. In particular, it was hoped to discover whether attitudes of teachers in the North differed significantly from those of their counterparts in the South.

3650 questionnaires were sent out, and 2615 (71·6%) completed and unspoiled forms were returned. Since many schools asked for more forms than they intended to use, and some incomplete returns plus 50 forms sent in too late to be classified were not counted, this figure represents a very high and encouraging response. Of the 2615 questionnaires, 709 (27%) came from primary school teachers, 695 (26·5%) from secondary modern school teachers, 904 (34·5%) from grammar school teachers, 259 (10%) from members of staff in comprehensive schools and 48 (2%) from staff in technical schools. It is perhaps worth adding that questionnaires were sent only to teachers working in fully maintained schools in the education service.

For relative ease of reference there now follow several tables which illustrate the distribution of replies in various ways. Tables 1 and 2 are concerned with the areas and types of school from which responses were received.

As Table 2 shows a larger number of questionnaires were sent to teachers in secondary schools than to their colleagues at the

49

TABLE 1

Area	Schools approached	Schools sent forms		Schools replying			No. of Q's sent	No. of Q's returned	
		No.	%	No.	%	% asked	No.	No.	%
Co. Durham	88	82	(93·2)	75	(91·5)	85·2	882	713	(80·8)
Bucks and Berks	81	62	(76·5)	53	(85·5)	65·4	571	444	(77·7)
Leeds	46	30	(65·2)	28	(93·3)	60·8	340	287	(84·4)
Portsmouth	28	21	(75)	19	(90·5)	67·8	241	165	(68·5)
All others	177	142	(80·2)	136	(95·8)	76·8	1616	1006	(62·25)
TOTAL	420	337	(80·2)	311	(92·3)	74	3650	2615	(71·6)

TABLE 2

Type of School	No. approached	No. sent forms		No. replying		
			%		%	% asked
Primary	155	129	(83·2)	116	(90·0)	74·8
Secondary Modern	122	96	(78·7)	86	(89·6)	70·5
Secondary Grammar	111	85	(76·6)	83	(97·6)	74·8
Comprehensive	28	23	(82·1)	22	(95·65)	78·6
Technical	4	4	(100)	4	(100)	100
TOTAL	420	337	(80·2)	311	(92·3)	74

primary stage. It was not thought that moral and religious education mattered less at the primary level than later in the school life of pupils, but that since greater questioning and analysis in these fields of study are much more common in the secondary stage, there should therefore be as full a response as possible from teachers of pupils in the 11 to 18 age range. As the figures quoted above show, a very satisfactory response came from all the schools approached.

The replies were also clearly representative of teachers of both sexes, of all subjects, of varied lengths of service in the profession and in all kinds of teaching posts. 454 respondents (17·4%) held posts in boys' schools, 487 (18·6%) in girls' schools and 1674 (64%) in co-educational schools.

Table 3 shows how the sample was constituted according to the type of teaching post held by respondents. The posts of housemaster or mistress, senior master and senior mistress, recorded in their replies by about 30 teachers, have been included under the category of Deputy Head.

TABLE 3 Teaching Post of Respondents

Post	No.	% of Total	Primary	Modern	Grammar	Compr.	Tech.
			% of 2615	% of 2615	% of 2615	% of 2615	% of 2615
Asst. Teacher	1596	(61)	19·6	15·7	18·6	5·85	1·22
Head of Dept.	589	(22·5)	0·65	6·0	12·2	3·1	0·50
Deputy Head	202	(7·7)	2·75	2·5	1·8	0·61	0·04
Head Teacher	228	(8·7)	4·1	2·3	1·9	0·31	0·11
TOTAL	2615	(100)	27·1	26·5	34·5	10·0	1·9

Table 4 is concerned with the length of service of respondents. Although fewer teachers of five to ten years' experience replied compared with the rest, the distribution is again very satisfactory.

TABLE 4 Length of Service of Respondents

Years in teaching	No.	% of Total	Primary	Modern	Grammar	Compr.	Tech.
			% of 2615	% of 2615	% of 2615	% of 2615	% of 2615
More than 20	679	(25·9)	7·9	6·9	9·5	1·4	0·23
10–20	752	(28·7)	7·6	8·2	9·2	3·2	0·53
5–10	495	(18·9)	4·2	4·9	6·8	2·4	0·5
5 or less	689	(26·3)	7·4	6·5	9·0	3·0	0·61
TOTAL	2615	(100)	27·1	26·5	34·5	10·0	1·9

Table 5 indicates the sex and marital status of the teachers who replied to the questionnaire.

TABLE 5 Sex and Marital Status of Respondents

	No.	% of Total	Primary	Modern	Grammar	Compr.	Tech.
			% of 2615	% of 2615	% of 2615	% of 2615	% of 2615
Male	1345	(51·4)	9·1	14·7	19·4	6·7	1·4
Female	1270	(48·6)	18·0	11·8	15·1	3·2	0·42
TOTAL	2615	(100)	27·1	26·5	34·5	10·0	1·9
Married	1764	(67·5)	18·3	19·3	21·4	7·1	1·3
Single	851	(32·5)	8·8	7·2	13·1	2·83	0·53
TOTAL	2615	(100)	27·1	26·5	34·5	10·0	1·9

Finally Table 6 shows the subjects taught by those respondents who were concerned with one particular specialism.

TABLE 6 Specialist Subjects of Respondents

Subject	No. teaching it	% of 2615
English	318	12·2
Modern Languages	175	6·7
History	171	6·5
Geography	151	5·8
Mathematics	227	8·7
Physics	103	3·9
Chemistry	95	3·7
Biology	100	3·8
Religious Knowledge	136	5·2
Music	60	2·3
Art	73	2·8
Economics	14	0·5
Classics	48	1·8
Physical Education	93	3·5
Domestic Subjects	94	3·6
Wood/Metal/Crafts	82	3·1
Rural Science	19	0·7
Commerce	17	0·6

Altogether 1976 teachers (75·6%) recorded their main specialist subject, almost all the remainder being teachers in primary schools. A small number of these also listed their subject, and these are included in the total of 1976. Occasionally subjects named were grouped for convenience under a general heading. Thus French, German, Spanish and Russian appear under

Modern Languages, Home Economics and Needlework under Domestic Subjects, and Technical Drawing and Engineering Drawing under Wood/Metal/Crafts.

As all these tables reveal, the replies were distributed in very satisfactory proportions in that no important grouping of teachers is under-represented. Therefore, the findings may be said to be fairly representative of all sections of teachers in the maintained school system.

SOME FINDINGS

One of the first questions asked concerned the proposal that special periods, not including religious knowledge periods, should be set aside in maintained schools for moral education. A number of suggestions was listed as to when in both primary and secondary schools such periods might be included in time-tables, and respondents were asked to tick those with which they agreed. Table 7 lists the options and the total percentage of

TABLE 7   Special Periods for Moral Education

Options	% of whole sample choosing these options	% of Co. Durham and Leeds teachers choosing these options	% of Bucks, Berks and Portsmouth teachers choosing these options
For all junior school year groups (7+ to 11+)	13·6	14·9	13·3
For the 10+ to 11+ yr. group only in junior schools	9·7	10·4	10·8
Only in secondary schools	7·6	8·0	6·7
For all sec. school year groups	29·5	31·1	26·9
For the 13+ to 16+ year groups	24·5	24·2	26·6
For VI form groups	22·0	21·8	24·4
Not at all	34·3	34·0	32·8
Uncertain	3·3	2·3	4·6

teachers who ticked each one. The table also includes the combined responses firstly from Co. Durham and Leeds and then from Bucks and Berks and Portsmouth, in order to compare reactions from teachers in the North and the South with each other and with the whole sample.

It appears from these figures that over 60% of respondents agree that special periods should be set aside for moral education in the maintained schools. This is true not only of teachers in the North and South but also of teachers in all areas of the country. These lessons are desired particularly at the secondary school level. On the other hand, Table 7 reveals also that there is substantial opposition in the profession to the proposal. All the returns to all questions asked have been analysed according to various breakdowns, particularly those described in Tables 3, 4, 5 and 6. A study of these breakdowns reveals that far more headteachers and deputy heads, and teachers with ten or more years in the profession were against the provision of these special periods than the rest of their colleagues. Male teachers also were more opposed to these lessons than female teachers. In response to all the other options the percentage returns in all the breakdowns of replies were similar to those shown in Table 7 for the whole sample. Thus it seems that it is the more experienced teachers and those in the posts of greatest responsibility who are most against the introduction of special periods for moral education. None the less, despite this important minority, a substantial majority of teachers desire such periods to be made available on school timetables. This factor is one of the most notable findings of the research survey.

A question closely connected with the one just described, stated that if special periods are set aside in state schools for moral education, they should be taken only by members of staff who are willing to do so. Not surprisingly the vast majority of teachers, over 93%, supported this statement. Immediately comes the problem: *which* member of staff should take these special periods? Again various suggestions were listed, the teachers being asked to tick those with which they agreed. Table 8 gives these options and the total percentages of respondents who ticked them. Again the responses from Co. Durham and Leeds and from Bucks and Berks and Portsmouth are included to illustrate the reactions of teachers in the North and South.

TABLE 8 Who Should Take Special Moral Education Periods?

Option	% of total sample choosing these options	% of Co. Durham and Leeds teachers choosing these options	% of Bucks and Berks and Portsmouth teachers choosing these options
1. The headteacher	12·3	12·2	11·5
2. The religious knowledge teacher(s)	17·2	16·0	14·6
3. The class/form teachers	16·3	17·7	15·3
4. All members of staff	6·2	6·3	6·9
5. Several members of staff working as a team	55·9	55·6	55·8
6. No one	23·6	23·7	23·8

Most of the teachers ticked more than one option. Apart from a slightly smaller percentage of southern teachers who ticked options 2 and 3, compared with the return for the total sample all the figures in this table are remarkably similar. More primary school teachers ticked option 3 than teachers from any other type of school, probably because the primary school is much more committed to the class teacher system. It would also be more difficult for team-teaching methods to be operated under the present organisation of these schools. The high percentage of teachers who ticked the team-teaching option provides another especially interesting finding of this research survey. Such an approach to teaching is still rare in schools in the United Kingdom but interest in the possibilities of these methods is growing rapidly. They might well have many advantages in moral education lessons. For instance a team approach would share the responsibility for these periods, and enable teachers with

different specialist interests to make their own particular con-
tributions. The teachers who were most in favour of this option
5 were from the comprehensive schools and modern schools, and
63% of teachers with less than five years' teaching experience also
chose this suggestion.

Headteachers were more willing to take part in these lessons
than their colleagues were for them to do so, but only 47% of
them, and 45% of deputy heads ticked the team-teaching option.
Perhaps they envisaged more difficulties in organising such an
approach than the rest of their colleagues. The same two groups
were also much more prominent in their marking of option 6
('No one'). In general, however, fewer teachers registered their
objection to these periods in this question than when they had
the chance to do so earlier in the questionnaire. The explanation
for this change was given by respondents in comments they
made at the appropriate place on the questionnaire, and in subsequent interviews with some who replied. Many felt that, having declared their antipathy to the original suggestion of special
periods for moral education, they would now assume that one
day such lessons would be provided. Therefore they wished to
indicate who, in their view, should take these lessons. Table 8,
however, shows that an important minority are still firmly
opposed to the whole idea. Answers to this question nevertheless
confirm the fact that far more respondents support rather than
object to the suggestion, and that it is the newest entrants to the
profession who are most in favour of special moral education
periods.

Many of the advocates of special moral education lessons have,
like the signatories of the pamphlet *Religious and Moral Education* referred to at the beginning of the chapter, urged that
such lessons be kept completely separate from religious knowledge periods. In their view syllabuses should differ, and direct
moral education should not be regarded as the particular province of the Scripture teacher. Others argue that religious know-

ledge lessons are the obvious place for moral teaching. A further question attempted to check the response of teachers generally to this issue by suggesting that if special periods are set aside in state schools for moral education, they should be unconnected with religious knowledge periods. 36·7% of respondents supported this suggestion, 41·7% opposed it and 21·6% were uncertain. In the various breakdowns of replies those most in favour of this view were teachers with less than five years' experience (44% of them), teachers in the South (41%), science teachers (41%) and grammar school teachers (41%). Those most against were primary school teachers (47%), teachers with more than twenty years' experience (44%) and headteachers (53·5%).

Only a small majority of teachers preferred these periods to be connected with religious education lessons, and the figures show a fairly even division of opinion. The number of teachers who were uncertain on this issue is significantly large. It is reasonable to assume that no large majority will emerge on one side or the other until much more thinking on the probable content and methods of such lessons has been done, and widespread agreement been reached about these matters.

A great many teachers, whether they favoured special periods for moral education or not, felt that the moral education of their pupils would be furthered if opportunities were created for the practical outworking of moral principles, especially if these opportunities were linked with the world outside school. This view was also supported by most of the teachers interviewed before the issue of the questionnaires and by many who took part in follow-up interviews after the forms had been returned. A question which raised this issue stated that many organisations provide opportunities for social service for children and young people, and that state schools should also provide opportunities for social service for their pupils. 83% of respondents agreed with this statement, 7·3% disagreed and 9·7% were uncertain. Only primary school teachers, with 76% in favour, and

E

10% against, had returns which differed clearly from the general response. It was then suggested that if the schools offered their pupils opportunities for social service, pupils should either take part only on a voluntary basis, or as and when expected to do so. 85.3% of respondents wanted the pupils to take part voluntarily, while 14.7% desired them to take part as and when expected to do so. In the breakdown of replies according to the various groupings little variation was found from the percentages given.

Other questions were asked concerning the content of moral education lessons, and all respondents, both to the questionnaires and in the interviews, had many suggestions to make about indirect ways of helping their pupils' moral development in school. Also opportunities were provided, and readily taken, for the teachers to give reasons why they supported or were opposed to special moral education lessons in maintained schools. Their views on all these matters are discussed in the next chapters. This research survey has shown, however, that a substantial majority of teachers throughout the country, in all kinds of schools, would like to see special periods for moral education established as part of the pattern of school life. Also a clear majority thought that these lessons should be organised on a team-teaching basis.

Much more work will have to be done to devise courses and syllabuses for moral education which command general agreement within the profession, if these teachers' wishes are to be realised. Such courses and programmes must help to meet the needs of the pupils for whom they are intended, and take account of the particular circumstances of each group of children involved. If they take their place in school timetables, schools will have to decide what else to omit or reduce, in order to make room for them. Effective teaching methods must be worked out for these lessons. All this will take time. Even so it seems fair to deduce from these research findings that teachers would be very willing to experiment in this field. The support for such work would be widespread among all groupings of teachers in all areas of the country. There are clear implications here for those involved in teacher training, both at the initial stages and in in-service work. Courses should be offered on the philosophical and psychological aspects of moral development, and such programmes must be closely linked with practical work concerning content and methods in moral education. Teacher education is essential if our schools are to provide effective moral education for their children.

REFERENCES

1. *Religious and Moral Education*, October 1965, 20 pp.
2. Ibid., p. 1.
3. Ibid., p. 3.
4. Ibid., p. 7.
5. JOHN WILSON *et al. Introduction to Moral Education*, Penguin Books, 1968.
6. *Education for Personal Relationships and Family Life*, Second Report, Gloucestershire Education Committee, September 1966, 63 pp., and *Education in Personal Relationships*, Wiltshire County Council Education Committee, January 1966, 10 pp.
7. A very brief account of some of these findings was published in *Educational Research*, Vol. 11, No. 3, June 1969, pp. 215–218.

Chapter 6

The Teachers' Case
for Moral Education Lessons

The research survey showed that a fully representative sample of teachers in maintained schools was clearly in favour of specific lessons in school on moral education. Some wanted these lessons to be started in the primary schools while many more wished to see them established as part of secondary education programmes. Two queries immediately arise. Why do teachers want these lessons and what do they think should be taught in them? Both these questions were quite comprehensively answered by the teachers in their replies to the questionnaires and also in the interviews conducted in connection with the research project. In the follow-up interviews, many of which were with teachers who had declined or 'not bothered' to answer a questionnaire, particular stress was laid on discovering why teachers favoured these special lessons. Many reasons were offered to add to those in the written replies, and they will now be considered. For convenience they can be roughly divided into four main groups. There are reasons concerned with the pupils' personal development, others concentrating on their social development, a group which relate to educational advantages and a final set which might be termed practical reasons.

Concerning personal development, most teachers made the

same points. They felt that direct moral education plays an important part in helping the growth of individual personalities. A mathematics teacher in a Stockton girls' school tersely stated the reason: 'These periods are necessary to satisfy the needs of developing moral awareness.' Also such lessons will provide useful opportunities for self-discovery. Several teachers thought this would come through some simple child-development studies which could be considered. Discussion and analysis of particular examples might well help many children to arrive at a clearer understanding of themselves. A young arts and crafts teacher in a Cornwall primary school stressed that 'concentration should be upon relating the children's problems to daily life and to moral issues, to foster discrimination and understanding'. Closely linked to this argument is a larger group of reasons which emphasised the opportunities for personal guidance which might come through these lessons. Respondents felt that helpful leads could be given through discussions and also, as one Berkshire schoolmaster suggested, through 'the teaching of facts relevant to moral questions'. He cited crime figures and information about social welfare work as instances. Others suggested statistics about road accidents, world hunger, gambling and drugs, and 'information about the facts of life'.

Perhaps the most frequently suggested reasons which might come under the heading of personal development were those which urged that direct moral teaching would help to clarify the pupils' own ideas and moral attitudes. One or two teachers said that children were 'incompetent to decide for themselves' about moral issues. Therefore some definite teaching was necessary if they were ever to make informed judgments. 'No child can arrive at a sound social and ethical philosophy through ignorance.' A Durham teacher wrote that 'too many children, whilst expected to grow up to think for themselves, lack moral guidance and yet have to face the over-enthusiastic destroyers of the old establishment who do not present many positive ideas on moral thinking'. He felt the schools should therefore give children the chance to think through moral and ethical questions in a constructive way.

Special periods for moral education should include teaching which helps pupils to establish a firm basis for the development of their own ideas. In these lessons they could indeed 'discuss the advantages and the shortcomings of present morality'. A science master in a Portsmouth modern school summed up the views of most respondents who offered reasons concerned with the personal development of their pupils: 'Moral education should be aimed at encouraging children to think critically about moral questions, thus giving them a chance to develop both their own moral standpoint and their own personality.'

Education in social awareness was also seen to be a major function of direct moral teaching: 'Moral education helps to forge links between people'; 'Morality is a social business.' A third from Reading saw these special periods as providing 'an excellent chance to study a wide field of social questions'. A Warwickshire comprehensive school mistress felt that much more time should be given in school 'to investigate human relationships generally'. 'Schools should encourage responsible attitudes to other people and to the moral problems of one's society.' The need to increase the social understanding of the pupils was stressed by teachers in all types of school, and 'to help them to behave responsibly to their fellows and to adults'. An English teacher in a large secondary modern school in Cornwall was one of many who warned that merely to moralise at the children would be disastrous. She thought moral education lessons would be 'useful as a genuine quest for enlightenment on how to deal with the complexity of social problems that man encounters'.

Some teachers wanted these lessons in school to help raise moral standards generally, both in the schools and in society. They believed that enlightenment on moral issues and their underlying principles would produce 'better citizens'. The head of a junior school in North Durham makes the point interestingly: 'Such lessons would help to counteract the effect of one or two delinquent children with the personality to lead, and also check the tendency for children today to think less of the disgrace of wrong doing and more of their cleverness in succeeding.' Approaching the same view from another, more unusual angle, an experienced head of history in a large London grammar school wrote: 'The expanding potential of sharing in so many more aspects of life these days leads to many more chances of making serious mistakes. Therefore young people should be given much more specific help than they are getting in school at the present time.' None the less, many teachers were agreed that any success at school would largely depend on the more influential attitudes their pupils encountered daily in the home.

Perhaps the section on 'social development' is the most appropriate place for one other large group of reasons. These are concerned with the connection between moral and religious ideas. That they are closely linked is generally agreed. But because some young people are very critical of certain religious teachings, respondents expressed the fear that 'anti-religious ideas might become anti-moral also'. To have separate periods for moral education might prevent this. This was the opinion of the group of Christians and Humanists whose pamphlet was mentioned in the previous chapter. In the response to the research survey both professing Christians and others were again in agreement on this point: 'Moral education will not be as easily attacked as religious education.' Several respondents asserted that 'moral development can be distinguished from religious and spiritual development'. Lastly, a Nottingham sixth form teacher said this: 'Too many teenagers nowadays connect moral behaviour solely with that one R.I. lesson. They have difficulty in translating Christian moral precepts to their own lives any way. This difficulty is enhanced if they reject Christianity or if the

R.I. lesson is not well taught. Thus separate morality lessons would help them to see moral principles to be applicable to real present-day situations in their own lives.'

The largest number of reasons suggested in support of specific moral education stressed the educational advantages of such lessons. One of the most popular views was that schools must educate 'the whole child', and since man is a moral creature, training in moral awareness is a necessary part of his total upbringing. 'The child's education would be incomplete without it. Therefore some direct moral teaching is essential, in the classroom as well as at home.' A second point made by many respondents was that the topic of morality helped to link up many subjects taught in school. Thus greater co-ordination of teaching could follow through the special periods set aside for moral education, and some of the subject barriers might be broken down. Again, many teachers underlined the fact that moral education goes on all the time at school, whether special periods are provided or not. Such periods would, however, 'reinforce the continuing indirect moral education of the children'. For 'something positive and definite should be done as well'.

It was often stated that special lessons would provide opportunities for different teachers to express their point of view on particular matters. This variety of approach would not only maintain interest but would ensure that a wider range of attitudes was discussed and considered by the classes concerned. Their outlook would be broadened and their understanding deepened. The danger of teachers 'giving their own subjective views as if they were objective' was admitted by a few respondents, but most people felt that this would not happen with 'serious, experienced, tolerant, knowledgeable staff'. On the other hand these lessons might well provide the chance to use specially qualified persons from outside the school, as well as those on the teaching staff. Many examples were given, including marriage guidance counsellors, magistrates, personnel officers from industry, probation officers and lawyers. A large number of respondents stressed the value of having married teachers taking these lessons, especially the married women teachers who have returned to the profession after their families have grown up. An English mistress in a Portsmouth grammar school wrote: 'I think that the wisest plan may be to have someone, or a team, from outside the school, especially trained for this work, who will come into the schools for this specific work – this would also avoid the danger of pupils accepting, perhaps without question, the views of someone they admire for quite other reasons.' She felt parents should be able to withdraw their children from these lessons if they did not wish them to attend. The opposite point of view was also stressed – that outsiders should be excluded from the programme of lessons principally because the teachers who knew their classes would have a much better chance of influencing and helping the pupils effectively. There is good sense in both these standpoints.

Another argument follows closely after the reasons of the previous paragraph. This is that these lessons will also create opportunities for special talks, lectures and films to be given on topics that would never normally be included in the syllabuses of the regular school subjects. Material relevant to moral education but not easily fitted into normal programmes of work, could be introduced naturally and in a proper setting. Illustrations suggested were talks on drugs, sex, moral philosophy, the law courts and approved schools (community schools), some elementary psychology and physiology, and social customs and manners. One teacher offered the intriguing suggestion – 'various vices'.

Two other reasons in this section are worth recording. The first one points out that in the class or group there is a valuable anonymity. Many pupils who would never initiate discussions on moral issues themselves nor even take part in such activities, would nevertheless be present in these lessons and could well learn much that might otherwise pass them by. With certain topics this could well include the whole class. Also in some lessons, for instance where particular case-studies were being examined, some pupils would be encouraged to speak out on ideas and actions upon which they would not normally feel free to comment openly. The second reason was put forward by the senior geography mistress in a girls' grammar school. She stated that 'many teenagers are looking for a new approach to moral questions – an appeal to their intellects rather than the same old behests, exhortations and stories that they have been hearing since they were toddlers'. The point she makes is important, as well as true. It is fair to ask all the secondary schools whether they would be ready to help their pupils in this respect.

The heading 'practical advantages' fairly sums up the last batch of reasons put forward by teachers in support of direct moral education lessons. Of these opinions by far the largest number related to teaching methods. Since these are obviously connected with the educational reasons just described, they will be mentioned first. Many teachers felt that if these periods were included on school timetables, then there would have to be much useful experimenting with various approaches. Team-teaching, favoured by a majority as the way to tackle these lessons, is an obvious illustration. Discussions, group work, special seminars and the provision of a tutorial system were all emphasised. Most respondents in favour of these periods saw them as ideal opportunities for establishing much closer relationships between staff and pupils. All the approaches they mentioned encourage more informality than tends to be present in most other lessons. One economics master thought that ideally a special room should be set aside, to which pupils would go during their moral education periods. 'Away from their desks, and seated in comfortable chairs, the class or group of children would discuss more easily and readily with the teacher involved ... The room could be always available for this purpose.'

Many comments refer to time problems. Nearly forty respondents said that special periods must be allocated since there was not enough time to deal properly (some said 'to deal at all') with moral education issues. Most of the teachers expressing this view taught in grammar schools, where syllabus pressures often tend to be strongest. There is so much material to teach in most subjects, it seems, that some other aspects of education must be neglected, even though with reluctance. Another reason advocated by both primary and secondary school teachers really makes the same point in a more positive way. They would welcome regular moral education lessons for their classes since they would thus have 'much more time in which to deal with children's problems'. 'This important part of every child's upbringing would then be adequately covered.'

This comment leads into the last group of 'practical' reasons to be quoted. These all made the point that moral education 'must not be neglected', 'must not go by default', or 'be ignored' in school. The provision of special lessons would avoid this danger. Some said the schools must give moral training because they thought so many parents did not. What parents do in this matter, no one really knows. Most teachers would agree that ideally moral training is best given in the home, mainly by example and through a positive family atmosphere. Not all children enjoy the advantage of a stable and happy home environment however. Also on some issues parents may be too emotionally involved with their children to be the best teachers. The senior mistress of a Co. Durham high school wrote, 'it would be foolish to assume that all children are necessarily receptive to family persuasion. Often the reverse is true, even in what would be considered the best family or home environment. Therefore the school, as a less emotional and more objective influence might well offer a valuable source of moral education either in addition to, or in place of, that of the home.' A few teachers said that what the schools provided would be 'the only source of moral instruction available to many children'. Others declared that only the schools could and would carry out this task of moral education effectively. Finally moral education lessons in school 'would ensure that *every* child was brought in'. All would be able to benefit.

As will be seen in a later chapter far more of the opponents than of the supporters of specific moral education periods gave reasons to back their opinions. Those in favour were usually more concerned to express their views on the possible content of these lessons. Nevertheless, the reasons they did offer make up a strong and persuasive case which cannot be dismissed easily. Their views, and the fact that they were a representative majority of the respondents in this nationwide survey, should greatly encourage further thinking and planning in the field of moral education.

Chapter 7

Material for Moral Education Lessons

Two questions were raised at the beginning of the previous chapter. The first one – why do teachers want moral education lessons? – was then answered. This chapter describes the views of teachers on the second – what should be taught in these periods? The question was first asked of a large number of teachers and student teachers interviewed before the structuring of the survey questionnaires. From their replies six of the most frequently mentioned suggestions were offered as possible options in a question in the national survey. These options were not proposed as alternatives, nor are they mutually exclusive. Some attempt was made to test the strength of opinion of respondents by asking them to number in order of importance those with which they agreed. Very few of those who replied ignored this question. This means that most of those who were opposed to direct moral education lessons in school, in fact numbered one or more of the suggestions along with all the other respondents. Table 9 lists the six options and the response to each, replies being shown as percentages of the total questionnaires returned. It will be noted, incidentally, that these options illustrate the four main ways – philosophical, social, religious and sexual (mentioned in Chapter 2), in which the teachers interpreted the word 'moral'.

TABLE 9   The Possible Content of Moral Education Lessons

Option	1st choice	2nd choice	3rd choice	4th choice	5th choice	6th choice	Total % of teachers choosing these options
1. Teaching about general ethical principles	48·3	18·0	7·0	3·8	2·4	1·5	81·1
2. Teaching about the law of the land	5·5	11·4	18·2	14·1	13·1	6·4	68·7
3. Teaching about Christian ethics	26·3	19·6	9·6	7·3	5·0	4·1	71·7
4. Teaching about sexual morality	6·2	15·6	22·3	18·0	10·1	3·2	75·3
5. Discussion of relations between children and adults	10·7	14·0	16·2	16·6	10·8	2·2	70·6
6. Discussion of case studies	4·4	4·4	4·5	7·0	10·2	21·0	51·3

Option 1 was decidedly the favourite first choice, and this remains true however the replies are analysed. Most respondents who numbered it, included it in their first three choices. Likewise option 3, though not chosen by quite so many teachers as option 4, figured prominently in the first three choices of many, often alternating for first place with option 1. It is interesting to note that many respondents who wished moral education lessons to be unconnected with religious knowledge lessons, would still include teaching about Christian ethics in the content of moral education periods. All the options were numbered by large percentages of respondents, most teachers feeling quite strongly about each one except perhaps the last. In only just over half the replies to the question was this one ticked, and in over 30% of them it was numbered fifth or sixth. Maybe this was because some teachers were not fully sure what 'case-studies' were. (It refers in fact to the study of particular situations or series of events, hypothetical and real, in which moral decisions must be, or have been, made, preferably in this instance by young people. It also refers to documented accounts of the behaviour (and its consequences) of particular individuals, on a given occasion or over a period of time.) Some evidence to support this surmise came from interviews of respondents after the questionnaires had been returned. None the less, all the suggestions save this last one were strongly supported in all the various breakdowns of replies. Thus the great majority of teachers, whatever their school, subject, position, sex or length of service, favoured these proposals for inclusion in moral education syllabuses.

Before moving on to the next question on the form, the respondents were asked to offer other suggestions of their own about the content of these lessons. Such suggestions were not, however, to be numbered with the rest. 14.3% of the total survey added a plentiful variety of further ideas, and so did the teachers who were interviewed. Their views will now be summarised. Again they have been somewhat arbitrarily categorised into three main groups under the headings: personal development, ethical training and training in social awareness.

PERSONAL DEVELOPMENT

In the first set of reasons on the subject of personal development, respondents were concerned with the growth of personality and the encouragement of certain personal qualities. In some lessons there should be 'some study made of individual personality', 'concentration upon the psychology of personality', to 'help children to know themselves'. 'Human emotions should be analysed and discussed', and pupils should be helped to understand 'what emotional maturity involves'. Also, from one London schoolmaster, 'an explanation should be given of the different mental processes of each sex'. A young Newbury teacher wanted material to be chosen which encouraged 'the formation of powers of discrimination, evaluation, judgment', while a Portsmouth modern school master wished the pupils 'to develop their own moral standpoint through being helped to think critically about specific moral questions'. The head of a Gloucestershire comprehensive school hoped that topics would be chosen which were concerned with 'self-discipline in their whole way of life', so that the pupils were enabled 'to sort out the best kind of life to lead'.

Rather more precise suggestions than the last ones just quoted but in line with what they had in mind, were those which stressed the discussion of problems raised by the children themselves. 'The content of moral education lessons should include topics affecting the lives of the children we teach.' Or as a Liverpool teacher put it: 'Specific problems that occur in the children's experience.' The deputy head of a Reading primary school wanted 'discussion concerning individual difficulties and failings' while a teacher in the centre of Leeds thought that these lessons should mainly deal with any individual moral questions raised by the classes concerned. Health education, many teachers said, should come during these periods with emphasis on general health as well as on personal hygiene.

ETHICAL TRAINING

A variety of suggestions can be grouped under this heading. In the first place teachers of all kinds in all types of school felt it to be vital that moral education lessons should include teaching about personal and social standards and values. They would wish consideration of the rights and duties of individuals and groups to be taken into account here. Suggestions included teaching about freedom and responsibility, the use and misuse of authority, tolerance, sportsmanship, and about the problems of materialism. Also 'teaching of a sense of duty', about charity

to others, giving and receiving, about the value of consideration and good manners worked out in codes of behaviour, and
'a study of the use of money – making it, spending it, saving it,
giving it'. Many would agree with the head of a Co. Durham
comprehensive school who listed 'stewardship of money, time
and talents, teaching about the responsibilities of privilege, and
discussions on what is responsibility'. An English mistress from
the Wirral area wanted the pupils 'to consider conflicts between
personal morality and general standards or laws', while a
Hampshire primary school master would 'show them how adult
behaviour influences children's standards'. A modern school
master from a Co. Durham mining village asked for 'discussions
on the differences in attitudes to moral problems caused by
education, family and social backgrounds'. Most of these ideas
were summed up by the deputy head of a London comprehensive school who wrote: 'They should examine concepts of integrity and honesty, responsibility and service, morality, right
and wrong, as part of a way of life for the individual and the
community.'

Numerous suggestions were also made about religious ethics
as part of the content of these specific lessons. As noted earlier,
nearly 72% of respondents wanted teaching about Christian
ethics to be included in the moral education curriculum. Some
would add 'ethical teaching from other religions', and still more
extended the option proposed by the original question to include 'a study of Christian teaching generally'. Other ideas
included 'an examination of scientific and religious truth', and
a Portsmouth modern school teacher of long experience thought
that 'older, abler pupils' might consider 'the grounds on which
atheists and agnostics accept moral values'.

A lot of teachers felt that attitudes to work should come under
particular scrutiny if a study of values were to be undertaken by
the pupils. As well as relations between employers and employees,
some suggested 'the ethics of business' and 'differences in moral

F

values in the world of work' as further topics. All the points mentioned are summed up by a young Stockton English teacher who wanted 'discussions on attitudes to future occupations as employees'. Other teachers wanted 'civic responsibilities' referred to, while others again asked for discussions on rewards and punishments, including those received at work as well as those in school. A few respondents wanted study of the values of mass media, citing discussions on 'the moral implications of films', 'moral values of the popular press and of advertising' and 'analysis of the techniques of propaganda'.

A number of teachers regarded the study of psychology, philosophy and logic, and politics to be helpful in moral education. The senior mistress of a Shropshire comprehensive school wanted 'the teaching of simple psychology, showing how the unconscious drives can upset a person's general ethical principles'. A secondary modern school master from Harrogate would introduce 'very elementary psychology for the older children. Thus we could explain the reasons for social and anti-social patterns of behaviour.' A few teachers proposed philosophy in general, not just moral philosophy, and a Portsmouth modern school master thought that moral development would be much helped by some 'general analysis of suggestion, and of fallacious reasoning'. Rather more respondents advocated the teaching of politics, suggesting 'the study of international law and political ethics', 'a study of moral values associated with national and international politics' and 'analysis of cases of topical interest engendered by parliamentary activities'.

Most common of all, however, of suggestions connected with ethical training were those recommending other studies of an academic nature. The history and development of civilisation and of different cultures was felt by many teachers to be central in a course of moral education lessons. Through discussion of 'the traditions and culture of the home country' and comparison of these with those of other nations, moral awareness would be

74

enhanced. Not only should 'different ethical systems and societies' be studied, but, according to a young Buckingham-shire comprehensive school teacher, 'also the effects of cultural and environmental factors on the morality of various races'. A Portsmouth grammar school head of department wanted 'an examination by research and discussion of the roots and development of morality within societies'. Other suggestions included 'teaching about the customs of other lands', 'studies of racial differences, and 'consideration of the relationship between ethical principles and the nation's historical and social development'. Lastly, a biology master from a Birmingham technical school made the point in a different way. He recommended the study of 'historical evidence showing the disintegration of a society or nation when moral principles are lost'.

TRAINING IN SOCIAL AWARENESS

The third and largest set of suggestions for the content of moral education lessons concentrated upon individuals and social groups in relation to one another and to society. In the question on content, one of the options offered was 'discussion of relations between children and adults'. Table 9 at the beginning of the chapter shows how respondents regarded this suggestion. In adding further views of their own, they were in many instances expanding this option to make it include other kinds of relationship. For instance many teachers would use up some of the time available for moral education lessons to discuss relations between the individual and society. There would be some study of 'the effects of various forms of behaviour on others', and of 'the demands of society upon its members'. The individual's responsibility to the society in which he lives should be considered, or 'respect for others and for self – the notion of living in a community, giving as well as receiving'. A physics master in a Co. Durham modern school would have his pupils 'analyse the purpose and meaning of life both as an individual and in a community'. Another northern assistant teacher, this time in a rural school, wrote: 'Basically children need to know the necessity for the caring for all in society to an appropriate degree. To know the effects of their actions and inactions on others, and thereby on themselves.' He would therefore have discussions on caring for others and on 'situational ethics'. A Leeds geographer wanted 'teaching about the structure of a commercial society'. A Birmingham teacher suggested that 'pupils should be helped to understand the nature of the society in which they live, this leading to an examination of social and anti-social behaviour'. Finally a French mistress in a girls' grammar school situated in an inner urban industrial area in Co. Durham wished to have discussions about minority groups in society, to encourage respect for the individual 'even if a member of an insignificant or unpopular group'.

A large number of teachers desired discussions to be held about the relations between children and other children, but the majority who added further suggestions of their own stressed that all the personal relations which children establish should be considered. 'Friendships', 'neighbourliness', 'the moral obligations between person and person', 'the study of other people' and 'training in consideration of others' were noted several times. The whole question of social conduct should be raised along with topics such as 'liberty', and 'the rights of property', and 'the changing patterns of etiquette'. Also 'the relations between employers and employed, employees and unions, between boy and girl, rich and poor, friends and fellow workers', with 'the amount of freedom that can be allowed in each case'.

Another fairly large group of suggestions stressed topics connected with marriage, child-rearing and family life generally. 'How to bring up children', or again, 'child care and parental responsibility for children' were not subjects to be dealt with only in home economics and domestic science lessons. Many respondents hoped that 'family relationships' might be discussed in moral education lessons also, along with 'the responsibilities of married life'. Thus, as one Sheffield English master wrote: 'Problems that arise along the married way from those of young parenthood to those of old age and retirement could be aired, and the pupils helped to form careful, unhasty judgments about how both parents and children should react'.

Some moral education lessons might be devoted to the study of famous people, especially reformers and missionaries. Suitable material could easily be obtained, many teachers believed, from varied biographical sources. The art mistress of a co-educational grammar school in Bristol said that much time could usefully be spent 'studying the lives of people who are particularly worthy of admiration'. An experienced primary school teacher from Swansea was more detailed, commending the 'discussion of the social ethics of past and present famous people and missionaries, deliberately bringing out their qualities of courage, unselfishness and concern for others which helped to shape the destiny of the world'. Certain characters from literature were also commended for consideration in these periods.

A further group of ideas strongly advocated the use of visiting speakers in occasional moral education lessons. Such people could explain their work, and in particular, tell the children something about the social services of the area and how they were organised. Civic authorities, social workers, clergy, doctors and 'special experts' could come to the schools to discuss aspects of their profession and the relevant ethical issues.

Many teachers wanted certain lessons to be turned into 'practical sessions'. Some of the time set aside for moral education could be used, according to a Windsor history mistress 'to involve children and staff in community care in the locality', and she instanced task force projects in London, and C.E.W.C. and Save the Children Fund activities. Other teachers proposed

77

series of visits – to old people's homes, hospitals, schools for handicapped children, community centres, courts of justice – this outside activities programme should be linked to the work done in the classroom lessons. A few teachers saw in these periods 'a good opportunity to introduce socio-drama', and an English master in a Farnborough school would use some of the available time to enact and discuss 'dramatic situations which serve to illustrate common "choice opportunities" '. All these various 'practical sessions' were regarded as useful means of reinforcing the teaching done in moral education periods.

Finally, over one hundred teachers who returned questionnaires, along with many others who were interviewed, would include teaching and discussion about topical social issues in the content of moral education lessons. Among numerous examples instanced were 'morality and the motor car', the nature of violence, crime and punishment, capital punishment, abortion, nuclear war, problems of drugs, drinking, smoking and gambling, study of man-management and education. Also mentioned were problems of social integration and of the underdeveloped countries, and studies of the work of organisations like Oxfam and Unicef. 'Reasons for anti-social behaviour at all levels' should be analysed, as should 'the use and misuse of leisure time'. One Portsmouth teacher said that 'a syllabus might be devised out of current local and national news, so that we could consider subjects like vandalism, aggression, housing, the old, neglected children and animals, and so on'.

The two topics which were most frequently included by respondents were 'the problem of drug addiction', and 'questions of race'. Interestingly, many who suggested these were teaching in parts of the country where these issues are merely heard of rather than experienced day by day. Because both are growing social problems, however, teachers felt that children at both the primary and secondary stages should be made aware of some of the key issues within their understanding. On drugs it was thought necessary to hold discussions on both the physical dangers and the likely social repercussions. On racial issues, classes should analyse problems of integration within a country and also consider the interdependence of people and nations generally. One Yorkshire schoolmaster wrote: 'I should like to see a detailed examination of contemporary conflicts in the world as seen through the eyes of all participants, which might if carried out in all schools save us from greater disasters. Education has a great moral responsibility here.'

CONCLUSION

There is plenty of material in all these suggestions for a detailed and interesting moral education curriculum. It is worth repeating that there was no thought, either in the list of options in Table 9 or in the suggestions of the teachers, of an either/or approach to the different kinds of work specified. On the whole the teachers have practical considerations mainly in mind. They show yet again great concern for the personal and social welfare of their pupils. This chapter, appropriately enough, ends with some wise words which the great majority of respondents would endorse. The senior mistress of a Co. Durham high school for girls wrote: 'I think it is important not to over-emphasise any one moral problem. Teenagers get very tired of the eternal discussion about "sex and the bomb" as they put it. It is necessary to show the immense variety of moral decisions which have to be made in life and the necessity for individual responsibility for moral behaviour in ordinary, everyday relationships throughout life.'

Chapter 8

Indirect Moral Education in School

The moral education of children goes on all the time at school. As they come into contact with others, as they learn to work and play and live with their fellows, so is their moral outlook and understanding affected. Various attitudes take shape, standards are internalised, behaviour patterns become established, character develops. As the pupils meet and react to the various demands of each school day, they grow in moral awareness. Many of the items which teachers would raise for discussion in moral education periods already affect the moral development of the pupils, especially questions of relationships. Consciously to consider them in certain lessons helps to reinforce or encourage that development in particular directions for the benefit both of the individual and of the whole social group. Some teachers objected to setting aside special periods because they said that 'moral education happens in any case'.

The first question on this subject put in the questionnaires to teachers introduced the issue of indirect moral education. In interviews of many teachers and student teachers conducted prior to the structuring of the main survey questions, many said that the moral education of pupils was most commonly achieved through indirect, incidental teaching and in other ways. They gave plentiful examples to illustrate their viewpoint, and the most popular of these were listed for respondents to the questionnaires to consider. As in certain other questions, some attempt was made to discover the strength of attitudes of teachers by asking them to number in order of importance those options with which they agreed. Table 10 lists the options and the response to each, the replies being shown as percentages of the total questionnaires returned.

TABLE 10

Options	1st choice	2nd choice	3rd choice	4th choice	5th choice	6th choice	7th choice	Total% numbering these options
Literature lessons	3·3	12·6	12·2	10·4	9·5	7·5	2·6	60·1
The study of history	2·4	9·0	13·4	13·6	11·0	6·6	2·1	58·0
Music/Art lessons	0·7	1·7	3·5	4·3	5·9	8·3	15·4	39·8
Social studies/ civics	5·5	20·1	17·8	15·2	6·9	3·8	1·0	70·3
The individual teacher whatever his subject	84·2	5·6	2·7	1·9	0·8	0·5	0·2	96·0
Games and sports	1·2	9·1	15·8	11·7	7·4	7·7	6·9	60·0
Positions of responsibility	4·2	33·2	15·4	8·8	6·5	4·2	2·7	75·1

Not surprisingly, almost every respondent felt that the influence of the individual teacher would contribute more to the moral development of pupils than any of the other options. Positions of responsibility again not surprisingly, came second some distance behind. Most of those who numbered it placed it high on their list of choices. Social studies and civics lessons also figured prominently in the top few choices of those who included it in their list. Every option was numbered by quite large percentages of teachers in all their various groupings, except music and art lessons which most respondents numbered last on their lists, if at all.

Teachers who were interviewed before and after the main survey took place were asked to say how the various options they chose contributed to the moral development of the pupils. Concerning literature the following comments were made. Literature lessons involve the study of life situations and of characters. Moral values also must be considered. Certain books might be chosen for reading because they would inevitably provoke discussion of moral issues. On history, respondents mentioned 'the approach through personalities', the need to make comparisons, the demonstration of causes and effects, methods of questioning, and the need to make judgments. Teachers felt that social studies helped by making the pupils consider their society and its demands, and the various relationships in it. Also situational explanations would be of more help to the less able children 'along with learning about communal living'. All the personal dealings which individual teachers had with their pupils would have a moral influence, many thought. Establishing and maintaining good relations with children helped greatly, as did the teacher's personal example. Many teachers pointed out that children have a keen sense of justice. If teachers showed a similar concern and acted fairly at all times, then much moral good would be achieved. The exercise of responsibility, however slight, was always beneficial in helping a pupil's moral awareness. Decision making and being trusted to do certain tasks was of particular value. Concerning games, most teachers stressed team-work and the personal responsibility to train and not let the side down. Fair play also was underlined. Lastly on music and art, standards were again mentioned, and several teachers commented on the moral value of criticising that modern art which by design has no message other than what the viewer sees there. Others mentioned the effect of art on both creator and those who saw or heard the results. Music, especially sacred music, some thought, increased the listener's moral and spiritual awareness.

When teachers had recorded their answers to the question about indirect moral education, they were asked, before moving on to the next question, to add but not to number any other suggestions of their own concerning ways in which indirect moral education might be achieved. 24% of respondents offered further options. These can be grouped under three main headings – various school studies, school community life, and the attitudes and example of the teaching staff. Before considering them it is worth noting what the teachers meant by the phrase 'indirect moral education'. They would include all incidental teaching and instruction in morals or ethical principles which take place as it were by chance or unplanned in other lessons and in school life generally. Also they mean all the values, attitudes and relationships in the world of school which exert moral influence unconsciously upon the pupils.

VARIOUS SCHOOL STUDIES

Many teachers listed other subjects in addition to those mentioned in the main part of the question. Biology, for instance, was a popular choice. One assistant, teaching in a Buckinghamshire modern school wrote: 'Being near to and being concerned with growing things such as plants and animals has, I believe, a great humanising influence.' Some teachers assumed that sex education lessons would be given by the biology staff. A Gateshead master referred to 'the inculcation of a sense of wonder and design in nature which comes through the study of science, Biology especially'. Also the biology lesson might be a good place in which to discuss the moral issues associated with heart transplant operations, euthanasia, sex determination and experiments to prolong life. Other teachers listed the other science subjects as having a part to play. The physics master in a Windsor school stressed 'general studies science teaching, and the devotion to truth essential to good scientists', while the head of a modern school in Exeter remarked that 'scientific law and moral law are closely parallel'. The biology mistress in a north-east grammar school spoke for all science subjects when she stressed 'science education, particularly in the carrying out of experiments in small groups, and in doing one large experiment in each class, everyone contributing to the whole'.

Other subjects listed included hygiene, sociology, rural studies, philosophy, current affairs, television lessons, and individual project work. Domestic science (or home economics) had many supporters, one of whom from a girls' grammar school in Co. Durham pointed out that 'it is a subject which is supposed to bring the school and the home close together. It is a subject which can be the most realistic of all subjects taught in school and is therefore a natural place for all moral education'. A number of primary school teachers argued persuasively in favour of free play. One from Reading said that 'moral education arises naturally in teaching children to work and play together'. Another from London stressed all the 'free activities' in the junior school. A young Stockton teacher spoke of 'free play in the infants' school, particularly in the reception class where children are learning to share and play together on first entering school'.

Over 70 teachers said that indirect moral education came in all lessons, especially, as several underlined, those which involved group, tutorial or discussion work, or 'the study of human beings'. A London modern school master noted 'any subject that makes a child more aware of his surroundings and helps self-discipline'. The head of a Leeds modern school wrote that 'moral education comes through happy, purposeful progress in any socially-positive activity relevant to the development of the child as an integrated adult'. He commented that 'this is not found often in traditional academic work by at least 50% of 13+ children'. His counterpart in a Wellington school emphasised 'methods of teaching which put personal responsibility upon children, e.g. social survey work, and field studies'. Many teachers mentioned the classroom environment itself and the daily class routine. A Portsmouth historian included in his list 'the competitiveness of the examination system'. Lastly, over 60 respondents listed religious knowledge lessons and school worship.

SCHOOL COMMUNITY LIFE

The whole life of the school community was stated by a great many teachers to make an important contribution to the indirect moral education of the pupils. The largest group of suggestions centred on questions of school organisation, rules, discipline and rewards and punishment. 'The way the school is run', 'a school's code of behaviour', 'the general standards encouraged by the headmaster and staff, as well as those set in lessons' were commonly cited. 'The school as a microcosm of society should illustrate the necessity for a certain pattern of behaviour for the efficiency and health of the community'. A Devon modern school master mentioned 'the school's social organisation – houses, tutor groups, voluntary service commitments, etc.', and other teachers added school councils, form periods, and the class unit. A respondent from Berkshire emphasised 'the manner in which school regulations are formulated and enforced, especially when the reasons for these are explained, and the children understand they are for the benefit of all, and not merely for the sake of making rules'. 'The involvement of children in planning school activities' was a suggestion from a Streatham primary school mistress, and others mentioned 'how responsibility is delegated'.

Discipline was stressed most of all. 'Good school and form room discipline helps self discipline', commented the Scripture mistress of a large Co. Durham girls' school. 'Kind, firm and fair discipline', 'the manner in which discipline is effected, and whether this makes for good or bad personal relations' and 'the staff treatment of delinquents or unhappy children' were all

85

instanced. A head of department in a Birmingham technical school added 'the public notice given to misdemeanours and why they are wrong', and an Abingdon primary school teacher suggested 'incidents of "moral lapse" which can be used by teachers to illustrate dangers'. As another Berkshire junior school teacher stated, 'moral education arises naturally in dealing with all behaviour problems'.

The second largest set of suggestions which come under the heading of school community life referred to 'school tone', or ethos, and to community spirit. 'It's a matter of climate and attitude,' said a London comprehensive school master. 'The prevalent atmosphere has great influence – due to caring, interest, sense of belonging and acceptance, etc.' A biologist teaching in Crediton mentioned 'the moral tone of the school – derived from continuity of example through the staff and succeeding generations of pupils'. 'School traditions' was listed several times. A modern linguist from Slough stressed 'a school's sense of values, and the fact that each person has to respect the rights of other individuals in the school community'. The deputy head of a Co. Durham co-educational grammar school summed up the point with the comment, 'So much depends on the school tone which in turn depends on the head, the stability of the staff, their team work and the systems of responsibility for pupils, all leading (we hope) to self moral discipline.'

The influence of pupils on one another was also frequently suggested as a means of indirect moral education. A Berkshire primary school headmistress wrote: 'The children working together, becoming aware of one another's needs and acting with courtesy and consideration each with the other.' A teacher of urban middle class children in Leeds suggested 'the association in school of children from all types of homes and environments'. From a girls' grammar school in Darlington one mistress emphasised 'the infectious general influence of certain individual pupils', while the head of the French department in a Norfolk school particularised 'the influence of upper pupils and prefects', adding the intriguing comment, 'even if at times it may be a fearsome warning to the younger ones'.

Many suggestions of a more general nature referred to community living and community relationships of all kinds. Items listed included 'working in a close, inter-dependent community', 'daily school life', and 'the fact of living and working together constantly'. As a Wokingham assistant teacher of geography explained: 'The social awareness of a community life must inevitably give a strong indication to the children of the moral standards acceptable to a community'. It is interesting to notice that of all the aspects of school community life only one teacher actually mentioned school meals. On the other hand, over 70 respondents indicated various extra curricular activities as playing a significant part in moral education. Discussion and debating societies, school outings, expeditions and visits (especially abroad), camping and field trips, social activities like open days and school dances, and inter-school activities were all offered many times. So also were numerous community service projects, of which the most common were helping the aged, collections for good causes, harvest gifts to the sick, the feed the minds campaign, and writing letters to sick friends.

There remain one or two infrequently mentioned suggestions which could come under the heading of school community life. Firstly there is 'the influence of visitors to the school, such as outside speakers, school governors, and other local civic dignitaries'. Presumably this further contact with the adult world has moral implications for the pupils. School counselling was cited by two or three respondents. They had in mind the specially trained counsellors, the first of whom are now to be seen in a few maintained schools. Several teachers felt that the school parent–teacher association had an impact on attitudes and approaches thus indirectly influencing the children's moral development. Finally two other suggestions are worth quoting.

The domestic science mistress in a Leeds modern school for girls noted the influence of 'illustrative material on notice boards, corridors, etc.'. And an assistant teacher with more than twenty years' experience in a northern girls' grammar school had a similar idea. She wrote: 'Flowers and plants – wild and cultivated. *More* pictures (of top standard) of all periods, e.g. Pissarro, Canaletto, Constable. Photographs of the great composers, musicians and literary men – any beauty in any way.'

THE ATTITUDES AND EXAMPLE OF TEACHERS

Nearly 100 respondents stated that the attitudes and actions of the head teachers and staff of schools contributed greatly to the moral education of pupils. A typical comment came from the French master of a small co-educational grammar school who wrote of 'the general demeanour of the headmaster and staff and their way of tackling problems'. References were made to the personalities of teachers, their personal integrity, their attitudes to their colleagues, their pupils and their work, and their behaviour when 'off-duty'. Most frequently stressed was the importance of the headteacher, his influence, approach and his 'talks in assembly'. One Derbyshire science teacher remarked: 'Much depends on the attitude of the headmaster to the importance of moral training balanced against his attitude to academic achievement and a smoothly running administration.' Teachers responsible for particular forms and classes were also said to play a significant role in their pupils' moral education. A teacher from a Buckinghamshire modern school spoke of 'the attitudes of staff to non-conformity, intellectual backwardness and competition'. Lastly in this group, the Scripture mistress in a Leeds girls' high school suggested 'answers to spontaneous, unexpected questions at odd times during the day when members of staff are available and approachable about the school'.

The other main group of suggestions which refer specifically to the teachers themselves, consists of comments about the personal example of every individual teacher. Respondents felt little need to elaborate this point. They simply indicated that how the teacher acts, and the kind of person he is, usually has more moral influence on children than anything else. In the primary school particularly, teachers affect their pupils in significant ways, and at any level real success will come only if masters or mistresses have gained the respect and co-operation of the children they teach. All the suggestions which come under this final heading are really elaborations of the most popular option included in Table 10 at the beginning of this chapter, the option which referred to 'the individual teacher whatever his subject'.

It is not always clear whether certain of the suggestions in this chapter really have to do with moral development. Nevertheless the comments reported above and in the previous chapter indicate clearly many of the facets of the teacher's role in the maintained school system. They reveal something of the complexity and the great responsibility of the teacher's task. They also show some of the opportunities to help children to grow to mature adulthood that working in school offers. Not least, they make manifest the many possibilities for assisting the moral development of pupils at all stages of their school life. Current research into moral education programmes and into problems of social interaction is indicating that schools can do much more, even in indirect moral education, than what has been very reasonably suggested by the teachers. It will be particularly interesting to see, as time goes on, how the profession utilises the knowledge and skills which such research makes generally available.

Chapter 9

Objections to Moral Education

In Chapter 5 it was recorded that over 34% of respondents to the nation-wide survey of teachers' attitudes objected categorically to the proposal that special periods be set aside for moral education in the country's maintained schools. Many other teachers protested against this suggestion in the interviews conducted before the issue and after the return of the questionnaires. Although clearly a minority they form quite a substantial one, and they are not confined to certain limited groups within the profession. The 898 teachers who made up the 34% who answered questionnaires came from all sections. Although, as was noted earlier, head teachers and deputy heads, male teachers and teachers with more than ten years' experience in the profession were more opposed to these lessons than their colleagues, in all the various breakdowns of replies the lowest percentage group against these periods was that of teachers with less than five years in teaching. Yet over 27% of this group did not want the provision of special time for moral education. Thus a sizeable minority in every grouping of teachers objected to 'direct' moral education lessons in school for their pupils.

The teachers' case in favour of these lessons has already been described. Those who opposed the periods were asked, in the interviews and at the end of the questionnaires, to state the reason or reasons which they felt most strongly supported their opinion. The 34% who recorded their disapproval in the questionnaires offered almost 2150 reasons in defence of their view. Of course many reasons were frequently repeated by different respondents. None the less, the case against 'direct' moral education lessons lacks neither variety nor detail. The arguments which the teachers put forward fall into four main groups, reasons connected with content, reasons connected with teachers, reasons connected with pupils, and practical reasons. It is in this order that these views will now be described.

REASONS CONCERNING CONTENT

173 respondents asserted that moral education could not or should not be made into a separate timetable subject. 'It is not a clearly defined subject', 'it cannot be learned in class like any other academic subject', 'it is artificial to treat it as a factual subject', 'it does not lend itself to formal teaching', and 'it cannot be imposed or taught in a vacuum'. These were typical views. 'It is too complex a subject to restrict to set lessons,' commented an art master from a mining village modern school in Co. Durham. A Leeds head of department of English suggested that 'to isolate it and treat it as a subject would minimise its true status', and his counterpart in a Portsmouth school wrote, 'One doesn't turn moral education on and off like a tap.' The words of a Bishop Auckland master admirably represent the views of many teachers in various parts of the country. He said: 'Ethics are a matter of social and value judgments which are likely to develop through the exercise of choice and evaluation in the pursuit of historical, literary and political studies. But I doubt that ethical standards can be passed on in the way that verifiable, ascertainable facts can be passed on. I therefore doubt whether it would be useful to sandwich 40 minutes of value judgment between say

91

a period devoted to mathematical fact and a period devoted to geographical fact.' His colleagues teaching English, music and art, for instance, would hardly agree. His view that moral education is primarily the inculcation of attitudes which 'cannot be regimented to a specific syllabus at a particular time on the timetable' is, however, widely held.

A corollary to the group of opinions just mentioned is another large set of reasons, over 130 of them, which claim that other school subjects or activities more adequately deal with the pupils' moral education. Alternatively, aspects of moral education arise more naturally in normal lessons and the general life of the school. As a Stockton primary school mistress wrote: 'Moral education should be a part of every lesson and every school activity, arising naturally therefrom.' 'All lessons are moral education lessons – good or bad,' remarked a Westmorland history mistress, while a Devon assistant teacher of English in a modern school thought there was 'plenty of opportunity within the framework of existing subjects and thus no need to get the subject out of proportion'. Another English master in a grammar technical school had this to say: 'The development of moral values may be likened to a skill such as writing: it cannot be delivered like a parcel of French verbs and absorbed in half an hour, but is a process of evolution conditioned by environment.' He appears to be opposed to 'direct methods' of French teaching as well as 'direct' moral education. Yet he would support the opinion recorded by nearly 120 teachers that moral education is 'of more value when it occurs incidentally', because 'on the spot instruction has a greater effect'.

Another reason commonly recorded stated that moral education is caught not taught, and that pupils acquired moral attitudes through imitation, and the influence of school tone. 'The ethos of a school should be the moral educator.' A Chesham religious knowledge teacher felt that 'morality is best not taught as a conventional subject but grown into, grasped and understood in a particular context'. 'In a good school unmoral be-haviour will produce a feeling of guilt at letting the school down.' Whether this statement is as generally true as many teachers would like to think is much less certain today than was the case some years ago. The attitudes of pupils, especially the older ones, to their school are changing. Most of them work hard, behave well and enjoy school life, but it may well be that the regard which they have for their school is less intimate, less emotionally charged today. To return to the main point of the paragraph, another Co. Durham science master of wide experi-ence argued thus: 'In a wholesome school environment, the contacts with adults of character, the friendships, and wide fields of knowledge opened up, should help to build lasting moral attitudes in a much more "real" way than the sham of holding formal moral lessons.'

One problem of content which caused a further large group of teachers to vote against moral education lessons concerned what they considered the adequacy both of material available for these periods and of possible teaching methods associated with whatever was taught. A geography master from Newbury raised the question by suggesting that 'without some form of Agreed Syllabus there would be no uniformity of content, and yet few are able to agree to certain universal moral laws which would be uniformly acceptable'. This view is debatable but he was by no means alone in expressing it. From Solihull, a biologist made perhaps a more telling point by saying that 'too wide disagree-ment exists about fundamentals and thus an *objective* syllabus is impossible'. Putting a different point of view about content, a primary school teacher from a rural Berkshire school saw these proposed lessons as providing 'too much scope for narrow-minded bigots, or alternatively the sheer waffle of the gas and gaiters brigade'. A Stretford art mistress felt that the content would 'vary too much according to the teacher taking the lessons, which are thus open to misuse'.

Establishing an agreed basis of morality was regarded as a real difficulty by certain respondents. Thus a head of department of an Aylesbury grammar school opposed moral education lessons because of 'the problem of the final arbiter. Or does the teacher preach that moral standards are convenient, comfortable survival sanctions, all subject to change and eventual decay?' A history master from the same school had this to say: 'To remove Christian ethical teaching and replace it with humanist teaching and then pretend that academic impartiality has been achieved is nonsense. Our society has no agreed basis for morals, and therefore state institutions cannot teach them.' Another history master from a London comprehensive school, however, objected to moral education on the school timetable because he did not think that 'a scientific and utilitarian morality should ever stand in isolation'.

Concerning methods, a remarkable number of teachers expressed the fear that these lessons would encourage preaching. Whereas in answer to questions on religion in school, only five respondents warned of the possibility of preaching, nearly 300 took the trouble to refer specifically to this danger in connection with moral education in school. Both those who favour as well as those who oppose special periods for moral education stressed that preaching to the pupils on moral issues was a real temptation. 'Moral education lessons would become indoctrination sessions,' claimed one Portsmouth modern school teacher. Another Portsmouth assistant teacher spoke of 'the danger of moral education being reduced to do's and don'ts if divorced from religious or usual subject teaching.' And the headmaster of a school in Exeter commented that 'isolated moral education becomes nagging'.

There were three other large sets of reasons concerning content which should be mentioned before concluding this section. All were connected with religious education. The first and largest group (nearly 100) argued that moral education could not be separated satisfactorily from religious education. Typical comments included the following. 'Moral education lessons are not necessary if the school provides satisfactory religious education.' 'Discussion of Christian principles inevitably leads to discussion of morality.' 'Moral and ethical codes derive their authority from religion.' A Birmingham teacher of biology asked: 'How can we define "moral" if we remove the basic justification for morality by dissociating it from religion?' 'It should be included in compulsory religious education,' stated an English mistress from Washington, Co. Durham, 'since this seems a more acceptable way of presenting it.' The head of a Devon modern school added: 'Once the question "Why?" is asked about behaviour, we are in the realms of religious education.'

A second, much smaller group of reasons said simply and bluntly that religious knowledge lessons were quite sufficient. The deputy head of a Reading school voiced this opinion by saying that 'since R.E. syllabuses make more room now for discussion of moral problems, so the need for M.E. lessons does not arise'. One other comment is worth quoting. It comes from the head of modern languages in a rural comprehensive school in Shropshire who remarked that 'in most people's lives morality is not divorced from religion, and to divorce them in school would be artificial, though it would obviously be made clear that some individuals and groups of people have a non-religious ethic'.

The third set of reasons, almost as large as the first group just mentioned above, emphasised that morality 'has no real meaning unless based on Christian teaching'. Said the headmaster of a Manchester school situated in an industrial area, 'It makes the whole thing meaningless if you divorce one from the other.' Another head, this time from a Yeovil school, thought it 'wrong to teach moral education in a spiritual vacuum. Our ethics depend on our belief', which for her is Christian. The deputy head of a Maidenhead school warned that 'morality apart from

Christianity induces the self-righteous attitude of the Stoic, the Pharisee, the Buddhist and the humanist'. Lastly a Retford grammar school master felt that 'without the definite basis of the New Testament, all moral principles dissolve in the seas of private judgment and relativism'.

REASONS CONCERNING TEACHERS

Almost 300 respondents to the questionnaires and 42 of the interviewed members of staffs included at least one reason connected with teachers to support their opposition to direct moral education in maintained schools. These reasons may be roughly sorted into five groups, the first of which, almost the largest, was surprisingly critical of the teaching profession regarding moral education issues. All these views were against moral education lessons because they believed the teaching would be so poor. A mathematics teacher from Darlington said: 'Some teachers would regard these periods as chores. They would then do far more harm than good.' 'How many of us are equipped to give inspired and purposeful lessons in moral education *regularly*?' asked the deputy head of a Berkshire primary school. 'I am not a Christian myself,' wrote an English teacher from Worcester, 'but I cannot see any source from which teachers of morals would be drawn,' and she concludes that 'the R.E. teachers would have to do the job.' 'Who is to decide,' demanded a French mistress from a Lancashire grammar school, 'which of us is morally good enough to give specific moral training?' A Staffordshire comprehensive school head of English has an answer. 'Teachers are no more able to teach morals than dustmen!'

It was startling to meet with so many denigratory comments of this kind. The head of a Leeds grammar school pointed out that it might well be 'difficult to find staff qualified by knowledge and inclination', and many other respondents stressed that these lessons should be taken by specialist staff. 'And where are they?' they enquired. One primary school deputy head commented that 'if moral education lessons were compulsory, a school might be faced with *no* member of staff *willing* to take them'. A Woking-ham assistant master thought it 'impossible to give such education without personal prejudice'; and the question 'Who is the *right* person?' worried many. Again many warnings were given about the danger of these lessons being given by 'militants, extremists, bigots, cranks, indoctrinators', and some who would have to teach 'with tongue in cheek'. A Durham English master echoed the reaction of many teachers at all levels when he wrote: 'If some of the R.I. lessons were to be renamed Moral Education lessons, there would be no let out for teachers. Yet what an awful responsibility to shoulder!'

The second group of reasons concerning teachers can be dealt with very briefly. These stated the view that the effect of moral education lessons was far too dependent on the character and personality of those who gave them. They therefore concluded that the lessons should not be taught at all. The reason given by a mathematics master from Houghton-le-Spring adequately illustrates all the comments made in this group. 'The effect the lessons would have would be far too dependent on the life and moral standards of the teacher in charge.'

This last comment is closely linked to the next group of about 40 reasons which concentrated upon the variations they said existed between different teachers' standards and in society generally. The art master of a Leeds grammar school, for instance, said that 'the pupils would be too much at the mercy of adult idiosyncracies'. The head of English in a Nottingham modern school suggested that the dilemma was insoluble. He thought 'moral adults are usually too moral and preach. Immoral adults are obviously unsuitable.' A biologist from Slough believed that if such lessons were taught 'by all staff, they would provide a legitimate platform for those holding views which are

97

unacceptable to society as a whole – and especially to the parents of actual pupils. This is most dangerous at the primary level'. 'Can you imagine', cried a Gateshead modern linguist, 'such lessons being taken by advocates of atheism and free love, or by left wing critics of the morality which prevails under the capitalist system?' Concerning the values of society, a Portsmouth grammar school teacher stated: 'Since our own society is so uncertain of what is ethical, moral or immoral, all that could emerge from such lessons is a vague, woolly discussion which plants even more uncertainty in pupils' minds.' This, of course, is one danger of any discussion lesson. A Chesterfield modern school master opposed to these lessons remembered Wordsworth and supported moral education after all. He asserted: 'And now I'm farther off from heaven than when I was a boy. Moral education should start with teachers, directors of education and ministers of state, in reverse order!'

A small number of respondents feared that the establishment of periods for moral education on the timetable would lessen the responsibility of every individual teacher for the moral development of the pupils. Some thought that 'the question of responsibility for such lessons would cause dissension on the staff', and others agreed with the secondary modern teacher who felt that 'if only some staff taught these periods, others might feel moral education was not their concern'.

The fifth group of reasons argued that moral education really came through the example, guidance and personal influence of individual teachers and the head. They thought that 'good personal relationships established between teachers and pupils were the best teachers'. 'The teacher's way of life should be so positive that his approach is a real example to his pupils.'

REASONS CONCERNING PUPILS

Respondents submitted a huge batch of reasons against direct moral education which related especially to the pupils. Most frequently mentioned were arguments which centred on the limited effect of these lessons. The head of history in a Co. Durham grammar school felt that 'specific lessons would make the pupils regard morality as just another school subject, possibly on an academic plane cut off from practical life'. Others said the teaching might be too abstract, artificial or too sentimental for pupils, and that 'direct teaching may create the wrong attitudes', since 'as another school subject it would lose its impact and benefit'. A geography master from Woking thought that 'making it a special subject would create an impression of limited application rather than an ingredient in all subjects and all relationships'. From a Portsmouth modern school another geographer said: 'It would inevitably become another Cinderella subject taken by a student or used as a period of time to subsidise other subjects in which pupils or teachers had fallen behind.'

Not only might moral education 'be regarded as something to consider from 3–4 p.m. and then forget till next week', but real antagonism might be engendered among pupils towards the periods. Many teachers argued thus. Said a girls' grammar school mistress from Darlington, 'children tend to resent being taught *directly* what is right and wrong and thus the gulf between "them" and "us" will widen'. Others thought that the pupils would regard the lessons as 'an imposition', or 'a joke', or 'a bore'. One primary teacher from a post-war council estate school in a Buckinghamshire town feared that 'pupils might become embarrassed and miss the meaning of moral education'. A Wokingham teacher pointed out that 'many pupils prefer to discuss moral problems with adults of their own choice', and teachers from Leeds and Bristol believed that 'if formal, then moral education can be tied to anti-school attitudes', and 'create real barriers instead of breaking them down'. 'Such periods,' said an East Anglia headmaster, 'encourage the feeling of being "got at", which children detest.'

Finally in this section, many teachers thought that direct moral education lessons would not really help children with their personal problems, and might even increase these difficulties. One north-east headmaster said it was 'difficult to give moral education in class without widening many pupils' experience to thoughts at an age when they were unable to cope with these'. Or as a young Woking chemistry master put it, 'too much self-awareness is not a good thing at this age (13 – 15) – there is enough already'. The deputy head of a midlands school in an industrial area thought that 'children may appear to accept the teaching given without really being in any way concerned, especially if the lesson is irrelevant to their own experience'. Many respondents observed that there were different levels of maturity in each class, especially at the secondary stage, whereas moral education was an individual business. Thus some pupils 'would not be ready for, or interested in, set information'. 'Learning situations for morals differ greatly from child to child,' said one Stockton primary teacher. Another from Hartlepool warned of 'the distress caused by teaching standards which conflict with those of the home', and a primary headmistress from Barrow wrote: 'There is no mystical content in morality – its cold logic can make no appeal to the deepest feelings and yearnings of children.' Lastly, a Bristol deputy head said this: 'We must not put unwanted ideas in their heads. There is such a thing as the innocence of children, and this we want to foster, and found their moral education (by indirect means) upon it.'

PRACTICAL REASONS

A great many teachers were opposed to direct moral education in school on what they regarded as practical grounds. One complaint reiterated frequently, stated that school timetables were too full already. 'Schools already have too much to do which is of a specialised nature,' said one science master from Stockton.

Others used stronger language. A Maidenhead chemistry master declared that 'the introduction of yet another time-wasting subject into an already overcrowded timetable is quite unnecessary and in many cases impracticable'. The head of geography in a Darlaston school exclaimed: 'What – still more extra duties for staff already overburdened by welfare work, milk, dinners, bank, dole award, etc.! When do we teach?' A Portsmouth modern school teacher was afraid that 'in an overcrowded timetable, this will result in R.E. versus M.E., or options between the two.'

Other respondents thought that weekly periods were of no use at all. A Dorset mathematician asked whether 'one odd lesson could outweigh the influences to which the young are exposed out of school'. Several teachers said 'the lessons would lead nowhere', and a further group claimed these periods would 'create artificial situations'. 'Children often say what is expected of them.' 'There are two kinds of child in each pupil, the one we see in school, and the other who goes home.' 'Children often stand apart when moral discussions take place, and if they expect moral teaching, they can close their minds to it.'

Almost 100 respondents said that moral education was the job of the parents not the school. 'The family is the place where moral issues can be most really faced.' 'The role of the parent is being eroded.' 'We should not try to usurp the prerogative of parents.' Such remarks were typical. An Aylesbury teacher of history commented: 'The place of schools and teachers in a child's life is greatly overrated, chiefly by teachers themselves. Some things – of which for better or worse this is one – properly belong to the intimate family relationships and outside social groupings.' An Abingdon primary school mistress remarked that 'some parents feel children are in many ways no longer their own when they go to school, and this would only aggravate that feeling'.

A few teachers thought that moral education was the church's responsibility. But the final large group simply believed these lessons to be wrong. 'Morality is a personal matter.' 'Moral education would be killed by isolation from other subjects.' So said a domestic science mistress and a teacher of rural studies. A classics master had dire forebodings: 'They represent the thin end of the wedge: the thick end can be Nazi Germany, Communist China, Catholic Spain.' He was by no means alone in thinking that 'moral education might change to political education'. One Stockton headmaster thought such lessons 'might well require all-embracing regulations, whereas needs differ greatly in different areas; thus such regulations would not deal adequately with every condition'. At a different level came the query from a head of history in a school near Manchester: 'How high a special responsibility allowance would the head of the M.E. department rate? Higher or lower than R.E., P.E., Maths? (So maths is more important than morals is it?). God help us!' Finally one more question, from a Birmingham technical school English teacher, who demanded: 'What do you want? Prigs, equivocators, sainted aunts? You cannot, unless you believe in Middle Class discourse as a dynamic teaching method, hope to deal with moral issues in an abstract way until the VIth form, and then only in small groups. I would wish to avoid self-conscious moral attitudes, narrow piety, casuistry.'

CONCLUSION

In nearly all the objections raised against direct moral education in school there is real concern, and most reasons were forcefully stated. The case made out by these replies varies in strength. There is no doubt that some respondents miss the point that moral education lessons are meant to supplement all the indirect teaching, not replace it. All the ways in which indirect moral education take place will not cease merely because one or two periods are set aside on weekly school timetables for more direct teaching and discussion. If the moral education of pupils is to be left to indirect approaches, will children in fact relate what they acquire to real-life situations, and to themselves? Some teachers would undoubtedly answer affirmatively, basing their reply on the knowledge of what happens in their particular school situation. Will children see the relationships between one aspect of moral development and another? This question, and the previous one, must equally be asked about the direct moral education lessons. If the teaching in these periods is well done, however, cannot we be confident that *all* our pupils will gain more of the help they need than they are likely to receive without such lessons? A fair proportion of answers tended to treat moral education as though it were an entity in itself. Also it was sometimes not very clear in what sense respondents were using the terms 'moral' and 'morality'. Some were thinking more of moral instruction about conduct than of moral education.

On the other hand the real problem of finding suitable teachers, properly qualified to take these lessons is a serious objection. So is the view that sees these periods as an encroachment on the role of the parents. Also the problem of having an authoritative, coherent, systematic and all-embracing moral code to teach (unless one based on Biblical ethics is adopted) is difficult to solve. Undoubtedly an attraction for many teachers concerning religious education lessons is that these have a definite, well-tried content the like of which they cannot fully envisage for moral education lessons. Will moral education syllabuses, when eventually devised, contain even the limited basis of fact found in most religious knowledge syllabuses? Fears of 'preaching' were far greater here than concerning religious knowledge lessons. Many teachers assumed that such methods were inevitable, in moral education sessions. Finally respondents were also right to stress the great difficulty teachers would have in trying to determine when children were ready for or receptive to particular ideas and problems.

Because they highlight certain fundamental issues, and because they represent the opinions of so many teachers, these objections are very important. This is why they have been presented at some length. They do not counter all the points made in the case for direct moral education in maintained schools. They frequently involve assumptions about how moral education is to be tackled which many of the advocates of more direct moral training in schools would reject. Nevertheless they posit real difficulties which must be tackled in detail before direct teaching about morality becomes a feature of school timetables at certain stages in the education of our children.

Chapter 10

Teachers' Attitudes
to Religion in School

If moral education lessons are ever to become a feature of the curriculum of primary and secondary schools, one of the main issues to be faced is the relationship between these periods and religious education in school. As was seen in Chapter 5, teachers were fairly evenly divided when asked whether religious and moral education lessons should be connected or not. A very small majority of respondents to the questionnaires wanted them to be linked, but many teachers could not make up their minds definitely on the question. A large number of those who favoured special periods for moral education desired teaching about Christian ethics to be included in the syllabus. Of all the reasons offered by teachers who objected to these periods, almost 10% could be called 'religious reasons'. As noted in Chapter 9, teachers stating these reasons felt that moral teaching either could not be separated from religious teaching or was better done in the context of religious education. On the other hand the research survey also discovered that almost all teachers wanted children to know about and understand Christianity. Many of these same respondents formed the majority who wanted to see special periods established for moral education.

There are undoubted tensions between religious and moral

education. One of the most obvious concerns the basis of morality, and the nature of the authority on which its sanctions rest. No agreement as yet exists on the relation between religious and moral education, either among all educationists, or even all Christians. That there are connections is certainly the view of many teachers who took part in the research survey. What they think about moral education in school has been discussed in detail in preceding chapters. They also have definite views about religion in the maintained school.[1] In an effort to focus more clearly their attitudes on both subjects, this chapter will centre upon why they wish the education of their pupils to include religious teaching, thus enabling comparison to be made between their thinking about religious education and their opinions on moral education.

SURVEY FINDINGS

The nationwide research survey, details of which were described in Chapter 5, revealed that almost 95% of respondents agreed that all children should be taught to know about and understand Christianity. 84% said it was part of the state day school's business to help with this teaching. 66% wanted state schools to continue to be required by law to provide religious instruction lessons, 24% disagreeing, and 60%, with 30% objecting, were satisfied with the legal requirement concerning school worship. Nearly 85% wanted the schools to continue to provide these lessons and 78% desired school worship to continue, even if the law no longer required such provision. Indeed 88% would like to see an act of worship in school at least once per week. 80% of teachers were satisfied with the present arrangement whereby pupils are expected to attend school worship and religious knowledge lessons unless their parents say they do not wish them to do so. Thus the present clauses of the 1944 Education Act still enjoy widespread support throughout the profession, a substantial majority continuing to favour even the compulsory clauses, despite the opposition here of an important minority.

In almost all the answers to the questions on religion in school certain trends were noticeable. Male teachers in general were less in favour and more against the religious clauses of the Act than female teachers. So also were teachers of less than five years' teaching experience compared with teachers with more than five years in the profession. Concerning the compulsory clauses of the Act, and also whether schools should provide an act of worship even if the Act were no longer to require this, teachers in the South were less in favour of the legal requirements and of the provision of school worship than Northern teachers. All these differences were statistically significant. None the less, the survey showed that the desire for the provision of religious education in state schools is very strong among teachers of both sexes, of all subjects, in all kinds of teaching posts and of varied lengths of service, in all types of school in this country. Also, satisfaction with the present religious provisions of the 1944 Education Act is general among respondents, however classified.

Certain points which were not mentioned in Chapter 5 concerning the replies are worth noting here. In the survey two questionnaires were used, in one of which all the questions on the religious clauses of the 1944 Education Act were worded positively, and in the other worded in negative form. For example, on half the forms issued, question 4 asked respondents whether they agreed or disagreed with the statement that 'state schools should continue to be required by law to provide religious instruction lessons'. On all the other forms the wording of question 4 was that 'state schools should no longer be required by law to provide religious instruction lessons'. Of the replies received, 51% were 'positive' and 49% 'negative' forms. One hopes it is hardly necessary to add that replies were not confined to members of staff with vested or emotional interests in either religious or moral education. The returns were fully representative of all groupings within the teaching profession and all shades of opinion, as well as of all areas of the country and of all types of maintained school. Finally, in the section of the questionnaires concerned with religion in school all save two of the questions were to be answered by registering a tick in the box of the respondent's choice from a five point scale, options ranging from Strongly Agree to Strongly Disagree with Uncertain being the middle option. The two exceptions dealt with why respondents thought as they did.

Why do teachers of both sexes, of whatever subject, of varied experience, of all types of post in all kinds of schools so generally want religious education to continue to be part of the school life of their pupils? One aim of the research was to discover the reasons behind the attitudes of teachers to religious knowledge and school worship. Therefore, as in an earlier survey of the attitudes of parents in the North East of England to religious education,[2] in one question six possible reasons why all children should be taught to know about and understand Christianity were listed. For comparison purposes most of these were the same as those suggested by the majority of parents, and respondents were again asked to add any further reasons of their own. Then they were this time requested to number in order of importance to a maximum of six, those reasons with which they agreed. Table 11 lists the six reasons offered, plus those who numbered each reason shown as percentages of the total respondents.

Here, as in the earlier survey, these reasons may very broadly be categorised as religious (1), cultural (2, 6), moral (3) and educational (4, 5), and by and large the considerable number of further reasons suggested by respondents also fit under these headings. That Christianity teaches right values was considered by far the most important reason, 41·6% of teachers numbering it first on their list, and 28·4% numbering it second. The next

TABLE 11 Reasons for Teaching Children about Christianity

Options	1st choice	2nd choice	3rd choice	4th choice	5th choice	6th choice	Total% listing these reasons
1. Christianity is true	27·9	8·8	7·9	5·5	4·6	5·9	60
2. It is part of our history	13·6	9·9	12·5	12·2	12·4	9·8	70·4
3. It helps people to be good	2·6	10·5	17·1	11·7	8·3	4·2	54·4
4. It teaches right values	41·6	28·4	10·2	3·7	0·8	0·15	84·8
5. Most parents want it for their children	1·8	3·4	6·6	10·2	12·8	15·3	50·2
6. National standards derive from it	5·2	19·0	17·5	13·4	6·7	4·8	66·6
7. Other reasons	9·4	4·8	3·7	3·9	2·7	1·2	25·7

most popular first choice was reason 1 on the above list, 28% tabulating it as No. 1. It is most interesting to note that all the reasons offered were considered by so many to be worth numbering. All in all, however, and in contrast with the response of parents, the teachers give the highest priority to educational and cultural reasons, with moral and religious reasons following behind, albeit closely. In the earlier survey this order was reversed. Respondents added a great many reasons of their own. Not all of these were numbered in their list of up to six main choices. Thus the total percentage of other reasons came to 31%. These reasons will now be considered in more detail.

EDUCATIONAL REASONS

Virtually everyone who agreed that all children should be taught to know about and understand Christianity included at least one educational reason among those they offered. A most important and frequently expressed view was that 'the spiritual development of the pupils is essential to their total development'. Teaching about Christianity is necessary in school since, 'it is an important factor in the integration of personality'. And a geography mistress in a school near London pointed out that 'education is meant to develop all aspects of an individual's personality'. 'It makes a vital contribution to the child's general education', urged a comprehensive school assistant master of much experience, and others argued that Christian teaching not only 'has close links with other subjects' but assists a child's emotional, moral and aesthetic development as well. A mathematics master from Windsor stated that 'present education is too biased towards the rational and secular' and he would agree with the young Stockton primary school master who added that 'the God-conscious part of man's nature requires nurture'.

The Bible 'teaches a definite attitude to life', it 'broadens the child's outlook', 'gives them a new dimension on life', and 'helps to form opinion'. 'It is necessary,' said a French master with ten years' secondary school experience, 'to meet the innate desire in all people to question and understand the fundamental problems of existence'. Many teachers stressed that teaching about Christianity stimulates the children 'to think and wonder and reason'. It 'develops critical faculties', and has 'a strong intellectual value of its own'. Still more pointed out that it is an important part of man's knowledge. 'It is vital to philosophy,' said an English mistress from an East Anglian grammar school, 'and in particular to man's knowledge of himself'. The headmaster of a boys' secondary school in Shropshire underlined its value 'as a means of self-discovery and as a means of evolving a personal philosophy and attitude to practical problems'. Many teachers emphasised that one main aim of education is to help pupils to formulate their own philosophy of life, and that Christian teaching plays a major role in this. 'It covers the whole spectrum of life in a compact unit', 'it helps pupils to understand the purpose and meaning of life', 'it is the basis for a complete way of life', 'it contains the basic principle of wisdom, where happiness is found', and 'it emphasises the importance of a religious attitude to life', were typical comments. A young

Newbury teacher praised its contribution 'towards the formation of a meaningful, positive and personal belief about the nature of life', and an Abingdon primary school assistant master saw much educational value in its concern with relationships and as an enquiry into the nature of reality and of life. Also Christianity provides 'a contrast to the materialism of today', a point often made by respondents, and according to a Buckinghamshire girls' modern school teacher of wide experience, 'it answers many problems which the pupils have'.

Over 150 replies asserted that religion, and especially the Christian religion, is a subject about which children must eventually make up their minds. They see religious education in school as helping greatly here. Such teaching 'helps children to formulate their own ideas about religion more easily when older'. A Berkshire teacher commented: 'Those who reject ought to know what they are rejecting.' A Bristol classics master excellently summed up this point: 'The main reason is that, in a society where all outside influences tend to bias a child against religion, a detailed knowledge of the beliefs of Christians and their reasons for holding them is essential if he is later to exercise a genuinely free choice as to whether he will accept them or not.' Or as a linguist from the Wirral laconically answered: 'Ignorance is indefensible!'

Lastly in this section, numerous replies argued that it is educationally necessary to teach a knowledge of Christianity because it 'helps to extend the range of our appreciation of this world', and in any case 'Education is incomplete without it'. Indeed 'it gives meaning to the rest of education', declared the head of a small South Devon modern school. And the head of a very small primary school in Buckinghamshire noted simply and tellingly that 'most children enjoy it and are curious'.

CULTURAL REASONS

All the reasons noted under this heading are educational reasons also. Many were commonly adduced by respondents. 'Christianity is not just part of our history,' said a grammar school master from Washington, Co. Durham, 'it is one of the most important elements in our culture, past and present.' And in that of Western civilisation, said others. It is 'an integral part of world history, current affairs and world morals', 'an important social phenomenon', 'a great influence in shaping the world we live in'. Knowledge of Christian teaching and practice 'is essential to the proper understanding of our society and its structure'. A Buckinghamshire comprehensive school assistant master remarked that 'it is at the root of much of our social thinking and institutions (Trade Unions, etc.)'. 'It is part of the children's heritage – of which we have no right to deprive them.'

Knowledge of Christianity is necessary also to a full appreciation of Western art and culture, and 'helps in the comparison of cultures'. It 'enhances our appreciation of art, literature and philosophy, especially that of Europe', and aids aesthetic appreciation generally. It has 'inspired music, art and architecture for centuries, and still does so'. The contribution of the Bible was frequently detailed in this respect. Not only was its value as literature stressed – 'the greatest example of great English' – but knowledge of the Scriptures is important since literature is steeped in Biblical influence. It has 'great story value' in itself, and it assists one's understanding and mastery of the English language. A Hertford grammar school head of department sums up: 'It is a source of inspiration, especially in the work of artists, for many of the finest and noblest actions and creations of mankind.'

RELIGIOUS AND MORAL REASONS

Over 60% of respondents suggested one or more religious reasons to explain their desire for Christian teaching in maintained schools. Only a brief summary is possible here. 'Belief in God is fundamental to life', 'Christianity gives meaning to life', 'Man needs a faith to live by', were much repeated comments. 'Christianity is a major world religion', 'it develops a reverence for all life', and 'it broadens the child's religious outlook' were others. There was a fair proportion of evangelistic reasons, and Scripture was often quoted, especially the verse 'Man shall not live by bread alone . . .'. 'Education must be based on the truth,' said one Leeds teacher, and more than one respondent urged that 'children need definite religious experience'. Perhaps the headmaster of a London comprehensive school should have the last word here: 'The purpose of all education is to enable children to recognize and choose the best when they see it; the best we can know is incarnate in Jesus Christ.'

Moral reasons were plentiful. Christianity was seen not only as 'a bastion against immorality', but also as 'providing moral and ethical stability' because its teachings are 'at the very root of a social way of life'. Being concerned with relationships, it is 'a good guide to individual and group behaviour', and helps to 'promote true community spirit'. 'It gives an awareness of one's responsibility to others', it 'encourages respect for others, and forbearance' and 'teaches the value of selflessness and service' by underlining the need to 'love thy neighbour' and 'to develop sound moral values generally'. A Reading modern school mistress argued that 'it helps personal relationships to be stronger since it gives a common purpose'. Others stated that its teachings 'help to develop character', and 'an essential humility', while a Leeds primary school headmaster noted: 'It encourages a conscience, consideration for others, and has a refining influence on children.' A history master in Barrow wrote that 'it shows them the true place of mankind in relation to his environment and other people', while many would agree with the Durham P.E. master who asserted that 'it provides the ultimate sanction for discerning right from wrong'. Upholding 'the highest moral and ethical standards', it is for many people 'the accepted common ground concerning moral values' and 'the moral codes of most western societies derive from it'. The art master of a modern school in Cornwall rounds off this section with the words: 'It is an important aspect of man's coming to terms with himself and the universe, and concerning his behaviour to other human beings. Thus it is a central part of man's development.'

PRACTICAL REASONS

Because it is difficult to categorise many reasons with any precision, and because so many teachers emphasised the practical value of religious education, it will meet the expressed intention of these respondents to summarise many views under this heading, although some would fit just as appropriately in other sections. Firstly, Christianity should be taught in school because 'it provides a centre to life' and 'is a helpful, steadying influence'. A South Shields teacher said: 'It gives everyone the basis (whether they use it or not) of stability, security, happiness, usefulness in their lives', while a history mistress, a head of department in a high school near Manchester, remarked: 'It contributes to a sense of security and emotional stability.'

A particularly common reason was that because many parents 'cannot' or 'will not' teach their children about religion, the school is the only place, apart from the churches, where children can learn something about Christianity. Also Christian teaching 'encourages stable family life', 'helps self-discipline', and 'enables people to live life to the full'. Again 'religion is fundamental to all peoples', and it is a good influence, notably, as a Leeds primary school teacher stated, because 'it makes people feel they matter'.

Why do teachers want their pupils to know about and understand Christianity? The head of a Streatham Vale school spoke for most respondents when he wrote: 'To educate the whole child, body, mind and spirit is our aim, and to provide an environment in which the whole child can grow to maturity. Christian teaching is central to both these tasks.'

REASONS FOR WORSHIP IN SCHOOL

Another question asked those who agreed with the provision of worship in school to consider five possible reasons why worship should be a part of school life, to add any further reasons of their own and then to number in order of importance up to a maximum of five, those reasons they most favoured. These were the same four options offered to the parents, plus a fifth most frequently suggested by respondents to that earlier survey. Table 12 lists them, plus those who numbered each reason, shown as percentages of the total respondents.

TABLE 12   Reasons for Worship in State Schools

Reason	1st choice	2nd choice	3rd choice	4th choice	5th choice	Total% listing this reason
It brings the head teacher and all the children together regularly	8·4	9·2	11·1	13·4	20·3	62·4
It helps in the children's religious education	6·8	14·9	22·6	14·1	7·1	65·5
It helps the community spirit of the school	13·7	20·4	16·5	16·6	6·6	73·8
It gives the children a sense of God	13·3	15·7	10·3	7·8	10·1	57·2
It gives all the children a chance to experience something of religious worship	48·0	18·7	10·3	3·5	1·1	81·5
Other reasons	3·3	1·8	1·8	1·95	1·3	10·1

Further reasons noted but not included in the five main choices, raise the total percentage of this 'other reasons' group to 14·5%. Again it is interesting to notice that all the reasons offered received considerable support. Like the parents in the earlier survey, the great majority of teachers, according to whatever breakdown their replies are analysed, wish all children to experience something of religious worship in school.

Analysis of the other reasons suggested by the teachers themselves, in their replies to the questionnaires and in interviews, showed that educational and religious reasons predominated. A brief sampling of these will suffice. Worship 'is part of our nature' and 'is essential to spiritual development'. It gives opportunities for all children to participate. 'All sections of the school can contribute', children 'can use their own initiative and skills' and thus understanding is helped. Also, as a Bristol teacher noted, 'all can share in the activity. No one is "good" or "bad", and no anxiety is involved.' A geographer from Ferryhill pointed out that worship 'can be a practical expression of truths learned in R.E. lessons' and others felt it could 'provide a bridge between religious and moral education' and 'help to make spiritual and moral issues relevant to life'. 'It helps the children to see themselves in proper perspective,' said a Surrey art master. A mathematics master from a school in Windsor went further: 'It demonstrates to the children that the superior adult world itself is not omnipotent and omniscient.' Many said that it was an essential part of religious and general education, and one experienced Worthing head of department felt that it provided 'an emotional experience that lifts the children out of their ordinary environment'.

Worship 'gives a *deeper* appreciation of God and his Truth', and it enables a child to get his priorities right since 'it is man's primary duty to worship'. 'It makes religion part of everyday living, not just something for Church, or Sunday.' 'It may produce the idea of dependence on God in prayer' and provides 'an opportunity for each child to bring his work and life at school to God', with his contemporaries. Again, as a Fylde P.E. mistress noted: 'It enables the school to bring itself and its standards daily before God.' It can 'encourage thankfulness', 'help create inner peace', and 'provide a spiritual bond between pupils and staff'. A Leeds modern school master stressed that 'children also learn to reverence all creation, and keep a sense of awe and wonder through worship'.

Other respondents stressed the 'value of this common activity shared with adults'. It brings 'a feeling of community belonging', 'contributes to self-discipline' and 'gives each child a motive to do his or her best every day'. Other practical results suggested included 'the enhancing of the tone, and atmosphere, of the school', 'the introduction of good music to the children', the chance to 'practise reading', 'and singing', and even, for one Portsmouth schoolmaster, the fact that 'community hymn singing reduces shyness!'

The minority who were opposed to the provision of religious instruction lessons and worship in school also stated on their questionnaires and in interviews why they felt as they did. The most commonly adduced reasons they gave applied to both religious knowledge lessons and school worship. Typical replies were that religious teaching was the task of the church and/or the home, not the school, that such lessons and worship were too inefficiently conducted, and that ours is now a secular society in which religion has no useful place. Some self-confessed secularists objected to religion anywhere, a few respondents thought religion was a subject for the fifth and sixth form stages, and inappropriate earlier, some said that worship was not possible unless the school was a truly Christian community, and eleven teachers feared possible dangers of pupil-indoctrination through these activities.

Repeatedly, of course, teachers stressed the importance of a proper spirit, careful, reverent planning, and effective conduct of morning prayers. Their defence of school worship assumes all this, and an encouraging number indicated that real attempts were being made in their schools to make worship meaningful and relevant. Others were very critical but from all they said one cannot but conclude that most teachers have very positive reasons for desiring school worship to continue. Let a Leeds grammar school mistress make the final point: 'It can touch the ordinary day with beauty and dignity. It can lift us into a realisation of greatness beyond ourselves. It demonstrates that reality is inclusive of the unseen as well as the seen.'

Thus, like the parents, teachers generally care about all aspects of their pupils' religious education in school. They took much trouble to make their views clear, and the real concern and insight they have shown can only be most encouraging and satisfying to all who have the all-round development of our nation's pupils at heart. The fact that many of them also want special periods to be set aside for moral education is not because they are dissatisfied with the content of religious knowledge lessons, although some have criticisms of agreed syllabuses. They acknowledge the importance of the moral and spiritual development of their pupils. Consequently they chiefly desire that more time should be made available in school so that more definite efforts can be made to contribute positively to both these aspects of their children's growth.

REFERENCES

1. These have been briefly summarised in the following accounts of the research survey:

   P. R. MAY, 'Why Teachers Want Religion in School', *Learning for Living*, Vol. 8, No. 1, September 1968, pp. 13–17.

   P. R. MAY, 'Teachers' Attitudes to Religious Education', *Educational Research*, Vol. 11, No. 1, November 1968, pp. 66–70.

P. R. MAY, 'Attitudes of County Durham Teachers to Religious and Moral Education, Part I', *Durham Research Review*, Vol. VI, No. 21, September 1968, pp. 285–294, and 'Attitudes of County Durham Teachers to Religious and Moral Education, Part II', *Durham Research Review*, Vol. VI, No. 22, Spring 1969, pp. 351–357.

2. See P. R. MAY and O. R. JOHNSTON, 'Parental Attitudes to Religion in State Schools', *Durham Research Review*, Vol. V, No. 18, April 1967, pp. 127–138.

Also P. R. MAY, 'Why Parents Want Religion in School', *Learning for Living*, Vol. 6, No. 4, March 1967, pp. 14–18.

Chapter 11

Teenage Attitudes to Moral Education

From the evidence and arguments rehearsed earlier in this book there appears to be a strong case for moral education lessons in school. It is a case commanding growing sympathy from teachers, parents and adult society generally. But what of the pupils themselves? Have they not a point of view? How would they react to the proposal? One is not suggesting that the content of a school's curriculum should be determined by the attitudes of those who are to be taught. Nevertheless if they have a particular standpoint, and older adolescents especially may be expected to have opinions on the subject, then their reactions should be known and considered since they will undoubtedly influence, at least initially, the approach of the pupils to any such lessons that they may attend.

During the early months of 1969, therefore, I made an attempt to determine some of the main attitudes of adolescents to the question of moral education in school. The investigation was also concerned with teenage moral judgments, and at the time of writing this chapter much work remains to be done before the research is completed. Certain results, pertinent to the subject-matter of this book, are available, however, and will now be described. They concern the views of a large cross-section of

14- to 16-year-old pupils in the fourth and fifth forms of schools in all parts of England. At first it was intended to limit the enquiry to about 3000 pupils in grammar schools and the academic forms of comprehensive schools. In fact an additional sample was carried out, for comparison purposes, of the views of about 1000 fourth form secondary modern school pupils who were in their final year of schooling.

A random sample of 140 grammar and comprehensive schools and of 40 secondary modern schools was asked to help by administering a questionnaire to one fourth or one fifth form in their school. Of the 180 schools approached, 136 (75%) actually assisted in the survey. 106 were grammar and comprehensive schools and the remaining 30 were secondary modern schools. They were situated in various parts of the country and served widely differing catchment areas. Table 13 gives a general idea of this distribution and also indicates the number of fourth and fifth form groups which took part.

TABLE 13. Respondent Schools

	Total	Boys G.S.	Girls G.S.	Mixed G.S.	Compre-hensive	Boys S.M.	Girls S.M.	Mixed S.M.
4th Forms	83 (61%)	14	13	14	12	11	10	9
5th Forms	53 (39%)	14	14	13	12	–	–	–
Total	136 (100%)	28 (20·5%)	27 (20%)	27 (20%)	24 (17·5%)	11 (8·1%)	10 (7·3%)	9 (6·6%)
North	41 (30%)	6	8	7	8	5	3	4
Midlands	32 (24%)	8	8	7	4	2	2	1
South	63 (46%)	14	11	13	12	4	5	4
Total	136 (100%)	28	27	27	24	11	10	9

The questionnaires posed ten fairly detailed questions some of which were based on replies given by over 150 young people aged between 14 and 16 years who were interviewed singly and in groups of 2 or 3 prior to the main survey. Completed and unspoiled forms were returned by 3651 pupils, 2829 of whom were in grammar and comprehensive schools and 822 in secondary modern schools. Returns were made anonymously and every attempt was made to reassure respondents that whatever they wrote would be treated with the strictest confidence. The forms were sealed and posted off as soon as pupils had completed them. The details which follow show other ways in which the replies may be categorised.

Using the Registrar General's five point scale for socio-economic grouping the replies are classified as:

I	II	III	IV	V	Total
254 (7%)	1062 (29%)	1534 (42%)	506 (14%)	295 (8%)	3651 (100%)

By rough geographical area, the grouping is:

North	Midlands	South
1054 (28·8%)	1094 (30%)	1503 (41·2%)

The breakdowns for sex and age of respondents are:

Boys	Girls	Fourth Forms (14–15 yrs)	Fifth Forms (15–16 yrs)
1816 (51%)	1785 (49%)	2262 (61%)	1389 (39%)

All these figures suggest that an interestingly varied cross-section of 14- to 16-year-olds was sampled in the survey.

The first question in the main part of the survey listed 10 objectives which many people have said that schools should try to achieve. They can be roughly grouped into aims which are concerned with the future careers of pupils, and aims centred upon personal development. Nine of the ten suggestions were also listed, with occasional variant wordings, in the Schools Council enquiry, *Young School Leavers*. Table 14 lists the percentage response according to sex, and, for interest, adds the response of the 13- to 16-year-olds to the Schools Council enquiry.

TABLE 14. School Objectives

Suggestion	Boys	Girls	(Schools Council 13–16-year-olds) Boys	Girls
Teach things to help you get a good job or career	96	97	86	88
Help you to develop your intelligence	94	93	–	–
Help you to do as well as possible in exams	92	91	66	67
Teach you about different sorts of jobs to help you to decide what to do when you leave school	84	89	74	74
Help you to stand on your own feet and to rely on yourself	79	82	66	75
Help you to widen your interests	79	82	32	23
Teach things of direct use to you in your future job	78	77	81	81
Teach you how to behave and make you feel at ease with others	65	72	58	69
Help you to develop your character and personality	64	70	41	51
Teach you about what is right and wrong	57	61	66	76

The second most popular choice in the moral education survey, (not mentioned in the Schools Council enquiry list of objectives), was included because so many pupils referred to it in the pre-survey interviews. The differences in response may probably be attributed to the differences of each sample and to the fact that the Schools Council survey listed more than twice as many objectives for respondents to consider. Nevertheless in the moral education survey, a substantial majority of pupils agree that all ten suggestions should be objectives for their schools.

In Question 2 respondents were asked to indicate which one of several suggestions they might choose if they had the chance to decide how to spend two to three periods of their timetable each week. The options offered, and the percentage response to each one are listed below:

1. Have more work on your favourite subject 8·4%
2. Have more work on your weakest subject 22·7%
3. Have talks and discussions on matters of daily life which interest you (e.g. how to behave, relations with others, what is right and wrong, etc.) 29·1%
4. Have talks and discussions about careers 16·8%
5. Have free periods for private study or reading 19·7%
6. None of these suggestions 3·1%

Item three, the subject-matter of which might be said to come most obviously under the heading of moral education, was clearly the most popular although options 1 and 6 apart, there is no great difference between the percentage choices. The different breakdowns of replies show a pattern which is fairly consistent with this picture. The one real exception is that of the girls' grammar schools. Of these respondents only 3·6% chose option 1, 16% chose option 2, but 38·1% selected option 3. A similar percentage for option 3 was recorded by respondents in socio-economic group I, 38·2% ticking this item. In contrast, about 27% of secondary modern school pupils opted for item 2.

The next question listed a number of subjects which might be considered in school in talks and discussions. This list was compiled from suggestions volunteered in the pre-survey interviews. Pupils were asked to think about each one and to indicate whether they thought it should be considered in school or not. Table 15 gives the details of the topics and of the response in percentage terms.

TABLE 15. Topics for Discussion

Suggestion	(a) should definitely be discussed	(b) Might well be discussed	Total (a) and (b)	(c) Should not be discussed at all
1. Friendship	15·3	71·9	87·2	12·8
2. How people should behave	25·0	59·6	84·6	15·3
3. The law of the land	37·4	50·3	87·7	12·1
4. Christian teaching about behaviour	16·5	52·2	68·7	31·2
5. Sex and marriage	75·6	22·0	97·6	2·3
6. Relations between people (e.g. between young people and adults, employers and employees, neighbours, etc.)	53·1	41·9	95·0	4·9
7. Family life	26·4	42·3	68·7	31·2
8. Standards of right and wrong	29·5	54·6	84·1	15·8
9. Rewards and punishments	14·1	58·6	72·7	27·2
10. Authority and how to exercise it	28·5	51·4	79·9	20·1
11. The qualities of a good person	23·0	50·1	73·1	26·8
12. The use of leisure time	25·7	46·1	71·8	28·1

None of the subjects listed was strongly opposed. While degrees of enthusiasm varied from topic to topic, it seems fair to argue that respondents generally viewed them all with sympathy. Analysis of the replies according to the various breakdowns on the whole reveals patterns of response similar to that shown in Table 15, with one important exception. Items 2, 4, 6 and 8 were all clearly more favourably regarded by girls than by boys, especially those from grammar schools. Balancing this finding, more grammar school boys than girls stated that these items should not be discussed at all. Concerning those who opposed items 4 and 7, Christian teaching about behaviour, and family life, two unusual facts are worth recording. Firstly about 10% of respondents went out of their way to explain that they voted against item 4 simply because existing religious education lessons already provided opportunities to examine this subject. On the other hand a surprising number of pupils of both sexes explained their objection to item 7 by stating their fear that discussions in this subject would be excuses for teachers to 'pry into pupils' private lives'.

Questions of sex and marriage and of personal relationships clearly rouse far more interest and support than anything else. These findings are strongly reinforced by an analysis of replies to the questionnaire's invitation to respondents to suggest other subjects which they believed should be discussed in school. A total of 1932 further suggestions was offered by just over half the 3651 respondents. Out of a wide variety of proposals, by far the most common (about 40%) could be listed under the general headings of personal problems and relationships, and moral matters. Linked with these are a further 8% concerned with problems of race relations, and 5% stressing the discussion of right and wrong, and of standards and values in conduct. Other well supported suggestions included current affairs (10%), matters of religion (8.5%), politics and government (8%), careers (8%) and educational issues (7.5%), the last group being mainly concerned with matters such as the running of a school. Money matters, war, social care, the future, home management, sport and hobbies were the other main topics recorded. One other intriguing comment deserves mention. A 14-year-old fourth former from a comprehensive school in the home counties wrote: 'I cannot think of any other subject of which to talk of. But I am sure my sister would like to have discussions about boy friends.'

It was in question 6 that the pupils were asked, as were the teachers in the earlier survey, to state their attitudes to the proposition that special periods (not including religious knowledge periods) should be set aside in school for moral education. The question tried to help respondents by giving examples of some of the more obvious activities which might be subsumed under the heading 'moral education', such as learning about the way people behave, what people are like as persons, relationships between people, teaching about right and wrong, and so on. It may well be, therefore, that most pupils in their answers were agreeing or disagreeing about no more than these illustrations. Yet because these topics would be central issues in any moral education programme, the deduction is fair that most respondents want special periods in school for moral education. In fact 71·5% of them agreed, 25·2% of these strongly agreeing, that special periods for moral education should be made available on school timetables. 14·6% of respondents disagreed, while the remaining 13·7% were undecided. Of those in favour, over 77% were girls (including 80·4% of respondents in girls' grammar schools), whereas just over 65% were boys. While these figures indicate considerable general support for the proposal, the sex factor significantly affects the results. Chi square tests, in which the don't know replies were all counted as disagreeing, reveal that the difference between boys and girls here is statistically significant. It is worth pointing out that what the teachers had in mind concerning the possible content of moral education lessons included all the examples used as guide lines in this question. One may therefore conclude that a substantial majority of both pupils and teachers favour the provision of these special periods and also agree about matters of content.

What reasons did the pupils put forward in support of their viewpoint? 85% of all respondents offered one or more explanations for their attitude. A total of 4892 reasons were presented and 4074 of these were in favour of moral education lessons. An examination of this huge group suggests that these reasons may be roughly collected under three general headings, reasons concerned with personal development, reasons concerned with social development, and reasons which raise practical considerations. It is interesting to consider what the pupils actually say, their generally frank and forthright comments providing informative comparisons with the opinions of teachers. A summary of their points will therefore now be made.

PERSONAL DEVELOPMENT

Under this heading four or five different sets of reasons may be grouped. One of these emphasised character and personality development. A Hove fifth form boy asserted that 'these lessons will help to develop individuality'. Many pupils agreed with the fourth form girl from a Nottingham school who believed that 'this sort of learning makes you a better person'. A 15-year-old grammar school girl from Retford strongly argued that as a result of such periods 'you will be more interesting, sophisticated, and nicer to be with', while a modern school boy from Fleetwood desired them 'because I'd like to grow older being straight, genuine and outspoken, and knowing between hippecrites and friends'. Perhaps a boy from Lyme Regis expresses the view of most respondents who suggested reasons of this nature when he stated that 'periods like this would help people to find themselves'.

The largest set of reasons which might come under this general heading stressed the educational necessity of moral education lessons. A Sheffield comprehensive school girl felt that 'moral education is the one subject we really do need to know about, not least because it deals with *us*, and people around us'. This view was commonly expressed by pupils in all types of school. A Leicester fifth form grammar school boy put the point very strongly. 'We are not here just to learn facts from history or maths or words in English, but to be able to live and make a life worth living to the full, not be like a cabbage.' 'It will broaden our outlook', 'prepare people to become adults,' 'because young people really do need help to understand all these matters', and 'because one of the main ideas of education is teaching behaviour', were other frequently voiced comments. A Saltash girl made a particularly pertinent observation. 'I think it is right to be taught the ways of life: at least if you make a mistake, it's not for the want of knowledge.' The frank reaction of one Co. Durham 14-year-old is also worth a mention 'Our education,' she said, 'is just facts and figures. If we had these periods maybe some people, specially myself, might take more interest in school.' And what about this impassioned plea from a Stourbridge girl? 'We *must* have these lessons because so many of the older generation do not understand human relationships. We should not end up this way – hating black people, prostitutes, drug addicts, Harold Wilson, and down and outs – hate gives you nothing. We should be educated in these matters!'

Another plentiful set of reasons – nearly 10% of the total submitted in favour of special periods – stressed the help that pupils would derive from such lessons both in forming attitudes and in determining conduct. Many respondents echoed the opinion of a Durham fifth form boy who thought 'these periods would help to draw up an individual moral code for each person'. 'These lessons would be a guide to moral decision-making and behaviour, and could well help if important steps have to be taken in these matters.' So writes a Salisbury 14-year-old. A Guildford grammar school girl made her point like this: 'Because if moral behaviour were discussed, explained and made more understandable, most people would see the point of it and would decide to behave in a better way, though not everyone would be affected like that.' Two grammar school boys, a 14-year-old from Harrow and a 16-year-old from Manchester speak for many of their age group on this issue. The former wrote: 'Because this trains one to be *capable* of taking the decisions of everyday life, not least between right and wrong.' The latter was much more laconic. 'Teach some boys manners!' was his answer. Pupils repeatedly pointed out in their replies to many of the questions asked in the enquiry that young people need wise and sympathetic guidance about many moral issues. They certainly do not wish to be told what to do. But they want help to sort out the issues involved in different moral judgments so that they can arrive at opinions which are balanced, and take action that is considered and sensible.

About 150 replies underlined the view that moral education was both interesting and important. Lessons would encourage more young people to realise this. Most of these answers were not very precise, although frequently expressed with vehemence. They recognise and acknowledge the seriousness of the many ideas, topics and situations they would like to discuss with sympathetic adult help, although one Middlesex comprehensive school boy desired these periods 'because they are important, because we should get pleasure at school and more fun'. One further large group of reasons (nearly 8% of the total) emphasised the need of young people for help concerning standards and values generally. Many pupils openly acknowledged their ignorance and puzzlement about these matters. They recognise the need for standards and are not unaware of the complexity of many moral decisions that they will have to make. They want assistance to enable them to clarify their thinking as far as possible. As a girl from Cumberland wrote: 'It is hard to know what is expected of you, and what is right and wrong, if it is not openly discussed.' From a Stockport fifth former came another reason, the first part of which was popular especially among the single-sex grammar school pupils who want moral education lessons. 'There has to be discipline,' he said. 'There has to be a line drawn about these things, otherwise anarchism will tear our civilisation to pieces.' The same point is tellingly made by a Wiltshire modern school girl who wrote simply: 'I think we should be taught to act like human beings and be taught right from wrong, so that we can teach them younger than us.'

SOCIAL DEVELOPMENT

The first group of reasons to be considered under this heading argued that special periods should be set aside for moral education in order that pupils might be helped to know and understand other people better. This was by far the most popular reason given by respondents, accounting for nearly 20% of all the reasons given in support of these lessons. The pupils want help in judging both adults and their own peer groups. They feel they could be given many insights into the different ways people behave and could also learn to understand why others act as they do. They wish to explore situational relationships of all kinds and to discuss them freely. Here, for instance, are the views of three secondary modern school boys, one from Salisbury and two from Lancashire. 'I think you must have some way of judging a person's behaviour before you leave school.' 'It is important that you should be able to conform to other people's views on morality so as not to offend them.' 'There would be a much better relationship between people. It would be easier to understand why people act the way they do.' An

Ealing fourth former thought 'it would give an understanding of all types of people without getting too involved', and a Middlesex comprehensive school girl wrote: 'So that people can learn about everyday people and their behaviour and what their real self is, as most of us put on an act.' The point that most respondents stressed was interestingly made by a fifth form girl from a Cheshire grammar school. She believed that 'learning more about people and how they go on makes one more conscious of others and more considerate towards them and one would begin to live as a community and not an individual all the time'.

Another set of reasons emphasised that the special periods should provide plentiful opportunities for group discussion and problem sharing. Such activities, the pupils believed, would increase social awareness and be very useful personally as well. Girls were particularly articulate on this topic. 'Some people have doubts about life and about others and this could reassure them,' observed one Cambridge fifth former. Another from Chelmsford thought that 'discussing such matters gives a less rigid impression of morals'. A third from a Surrey girls' school said that 'these discussions should be promoted to help our understanding of society. What is more, I often feel refreshed if I can discuss my troubles and opinions on certain subjects.' Finally, here is a clarion cry from Yorkshire. 'It is extremely important for us, the suppressed school girls, to have a chance to talk over vital issues to find out the truth. Through discussion and understanding we can become freer in mind, and can become more relaxed.'

Three other groups of reasons deserve a brief mention. Just over 100 reasons were stated which underlined the value of moral education lessons in helping pupils to understand the nature of friendship. These respondents felt they would be enabled to evaluate the responsibilities involved and also to choose their future companions more wisely. A smaller group of pupils believed that some of the special periods should be devoted to discussions about marriage relationships and family life, with their specific moral requirements. They would thus be better equipped as husbands or wives, and as parents. The third group thought that moral education lessons would equip pupils to become better citizens. By 'better' they usually meant more law-abiding and more socially aware and responsible. One comment from this group, perhaps worth recording, is that of a 14-year-old from Hastings whose reason was: 'For the sake of future citizenship, this is important, because the country is going to pot, and friendliness is dying out.'

PRACTICAL CONSIDERATIONS

Under this heading are grouped a large number of reasons, some of which might well have been more appropriately placed under one of the two earlier headings. Often the wording of answers was rather vague. For instance well over 200 replies suggested that the knowledge gained in moral education lessons would be useful or necessary. Another group of 288 reasons stated that these periods would be 'helpful to later life'. Rarely was a fuller explanation given although one fifth former from Rugby said that the knowledge he would gain would enable him to think for himself, while a Grantham secondary modern school boy made the perceptive comment that the useful information to be imparted would give him a greater feeling of security when he had left school.

Three other sets of reasons may be usefully considered together. 141 respondents emphasised current ignorance about moral issues which special lessons would help to dispel. A further 121 believed that these periods would help to prevent many pupils running into difficulties later in life, because certain problems would no longer pose much trouble. One Peterborough girl wrote: 'Moral education in school will prevent people from setting about finding out in other ways which may have disasterous results.' From Stourbridge a 16-year-old girl argued that 'there might not be so much conflict between generations if there was understanding about each other's moral code', and a boy from a Liverpool comprehensive school said that 'moral education can well stem the advance of decadence that always accompanies peace and materialism. It would encourage people to stop and think about morality rather than plunging along headlong.' The third set of reasons of this kind, 80 of them, claimed that the special periods would, in the expressive phrase of one boy, 'prevent hoodalism'. In other words, here is a solution to the problem of hoodlums and vandalism.

About 90 respondents saw these lessons as having vocational importance. Not only would the knowledge help them, they believed, to obtain jobs, it would also ease relationships within the world of work. Another 103 declared that too many parents cannot or will not provide effective moral education in the home. They may be reluctant to discuss some matters and 'can't always say what they mean'. Some do not have, or will not find, the time to talk to their children, while others do not always understand their families. It is not always that parents are inadequate. 'Young people are often reluctant to discuss these things with their parents.' For 102 respondents at least, the obverse side of this coin is that special periods for moral education must be provided in school since the school is the best, and too often the only place where pupils may receive such guidance.

Two very small sets of reasons deserve a mention. Twenty-two respondents said that moral education lessons would make a welcome change from the usual teaching. 'They would brighten up the timetable,' suggested one Gosport fifth former. 'They would relieve tension of other lessons,' thought a fourth form Nottingham boy. Or as another grammar school boy from Lancashire remarked: 'They are needed to break the week's lessons and to give you an interest and something to look forward to when struggling through hard lessons.' Last of all, seven pupils thought that these periods would be helpful to teachers. They would learn more about their pupils and the views young people hold, and 'bring them closer to the problems of youth'. Consequently they would be able to form more balanced judgments of young people.

OBJECTIONS TO SPECIAL PERIODS

A total of 818 reasons was put forward opposing special moral education lessons in school. Over 200 of these disagreed because morality was something personal and private and therefore not to be discussed openly in a classroom setting. Moral standards were an individual matter and 'you don't need other people to tell you how to run your life'. As a Hampstead 16-year-old defined it: 'Morals are what other people want you to do, not what you want to do.' Or take the laconic view of a Huntingdon boy who simply stated: 'I don't like being programmed.' A further 115 reasons pointed out that there was really no time in school for moral education. School was concerned with other (i.e. more important) matters, 'Other subjects could and would suffer,' wrote an Ashington pupil, 'if this happened. Another weak subject would develop.' There was a genuine fear that other studies would suffer if their teaching time were reduced. 'School is for learning facts, not moral education,' was the comment of a Westmorland pupil. A boy from Hove was even more succinct. He wrote: 'School is for *learning*.'

Seventy-six pupils said that moral education was the task of the home, not the school. Sixty-one felt such teaching was satisfactorily catered for in religious education lessons, the proper place for this work. Small groups of answers objected to these periods because they were or would be boring, useless, a waste of time or unnecessary. Over 80 pupils thought that moral education was acquired from everyday experience not from the class-room, whereas 40 others felt that such teaching was too difficult to attempt in school. A few thought that moral education was the job of the church, others the task of the English teachers. Nine boys and two girls, all from grammar schools, feared that the teaching would be 'too biassed', with only one point of view, the teacher's, receiving prominence. Thirty-six respondents argued that these lessons might do more harm than good. They might prove embarrassing to some people, or even offensive. 'If some teachers taught what and what not to do, we might all end up without individuality.' 'Many people discard moral standards because of the inward instinct to rebel. If this were taught in school it would seem more authorised and could make matters worse.' (From Salisbury and West Kirby.) And from Doncaster: 'Most people would just laze around.'

On balance the objections to moral education lessons were expressed as forcefully as the arguments in favour. Many pupils underlined their view that the approach should be open-ended, with the emphasis on discussion rather than instruction. They wanted guidance, not methods designed to compel or induce conformity. Dictation about standards, and preaching, were attacked. Teachers should encourage proper dialogue and provide the necessary information. One cannot fail to be moved by the earnestness and sincerity of respondents, not to mention their sensible approach to the question. To say no more, their answers reveal a great deal about the responsibilities and the privileges of teaching.

To conclude this chapter, the answers to one further question should be recorded. This raised the issue of who was to take the special periods for moral education, assuming that room was made on school timetables for these lessons. Various suggestions were listed and respondents were asked to tick those with which they agreed. Their percentage response to each suggestion is set out below:

Suggestion	%
1. The headteacher	7·7
2. The religious knowledge teacher(s)	17·0
3. The class/form teachers	14·7
4. All members of staff	11·6
5. Several members of staff working as a team	23·0
6. A special member of staff who does not take you for other lessons	16·6
7. Someone not on the staff of your school	40·6

These choices total more than 100% since some pupils opted for more than one suggestion. Option 7 was easily the most popular choice, especially among girls, 47·6% ticking this option as compared with 34% of boys. This difference, by chi square calculation, is statistically significant. Next in popularity was option 5, which was numbered first choice by the teachers when they were asked this question. More fifth form pupils (27%) ticked this than fourth formers (20%), while 27·7% of girls' grammar school respondents selected it, contrasted with only 17·5% of secondary modern school pupils. Of the other options, 13% of secondary modern school pupils and 13% of socio-economic group V chose the first suggestion, whereas only 2·5% of girls' grammar school pupils wanted head teachers to take part in moral education lessons. In all other respects, the breakdown analyses of replies showed patterns of response closely similar to that of the total sample.

70% of respondents said that they did have talks and discussion in school on such topics as matters of behaviour, relationships with others, and questions of right and wrong, but in most cases, these were occasional happenings, which usually took place in religious education, and sometimes in English lessons. Only 8% of respondents indicated that they attended lessons specially set aside for these discussions. It would be wrong to claim that the 3651 respondents to this moral education questionnaire were a fully representative sample of the nation's 14- to 16-year-olds. They do, however, form an interesting cross-section of opinion which demonstrates remarkable agreement, and their views undoubtedly reinforce the case for more specific moral education in school.

dards and values. Another task is to help pupils to assess these standards and values, to criticise and evaluate, not merely passively to accept. The Eppels argue that 'the most fundamental aspect of moral development consists not in unwilling adherence to a set of rules and regulations but in the building and strengthening of positive sentiments for people and ideals'. They add that 'this is particularly relevant in a situation where we can no longer assume a stable, organised system that will govern behaviour and affect even those who feel impelled to deviate'.[1]

If by this last remark they mean that our society's standards are unstable and disorganised, or that there is no stable, organised system available that can govern behaviour, they would have to produce much more evidence to reinforce their opinion. But most people would agree with their first statement. The problem is: what are these positive sentiments, and how can we build and strengthen them in the minds of young people? Berkowitz makes the relevant comment on sanctions that 'Our society . . . seeks to develop strong inner controls in its members so that they can police their own actions without the threat of externally imposed sanctions. Contrary to this ideal, research findings indicate that external conditions often influence the extent to which people in our society conform to moral codes. Their moral behaviour depends on more than just their internal standards.'[2] He is speaking of American society yet his words are equally relevant to the United Kingdom and elsewhere. Human beings, it seems, are unable to dispense with external codes of conduct with their attendant rewards and punishments. Rules and regulations cannot therefore be ignored entirely in moral education programmes. Indeed, as was noted in Chapter 3, they are essential in assisting moral development.

Some people want moral education lessons to help do away with the need for such sets of rules. They believe that with proper teaching and guidance, people can be educated out of any dependence on an external moral code. They think that through education it should be possible for individuals to internalise the best that a moral code can give, and that rational, responsible behaviour will inevitably result. Consequently such individuals might dispense with rules of conduct entirely. Such a view places considerable faith both in the power of education and in human nature, faith which up to the present time can hardly be said to be justified. For education, no matter how effective, can only make people aware of the choices before them. No matter how clear an understanding of each situation is given, it cannot *empower* any individual to select the good and reject the bad, to do what is right and to avoid the wrong (whatever one means by these terms). We cannot expect even the most morally mature person always to act in rational, altruistic, responsible and right ways.

There are other people, however, who believe that the evidence of man's need to rely at least to some extent on an external moral code is one proof of a fundamental need in human nature. They might well add that because man is as he is, this need will always be basic to his situation. The events of history and the current situation in all countries both suggest that they are right. They could go on to argue that moral education is essential for all not least to make people aware of this fact of their nature and to help them to understand its implications for their daily lives.

One of the chief reasons why it is necessary to present children with a clear moral code in moral education lessons, as well as discussing the ethical principles behind such a system, is mentioned by R. S. Peters, though he is speaking in a different context: 'It may be that, psychologically speaking, people are much more prone to take account of self-regarding than of other-regarding alternatives. But psychologically speaking they may also be more inclined to go for alternatives that are immediately attractive than for those that have qualities in virtue of which they are worthwhile. To correct such psychological proclivities is one of the basic tasks of moral education.'[3] Peters does emphasise elsewhere that teachers must insist that pupils observe certain basic moral rules.

In Chapter 4 it was suggested that the teachers as moral educators have three main spheres of influence – through the teaching of subjects, through concern for pupil behaviour, and through personal example. They have real opportunities to guide and help their pupils. Unfortunately, teachers are sometimes limited people, limited through their formal education and lack of experience of the world of work into which most of their pupils will go. Progression from school to college or university, to professional training and then back to school means that a fair proportion of teachers will not be able exactly to appreciate all the ideals, values and problems of every section of adult society. Some will be completely unaware of the moral issues which face many of their children on leaving school.

It is in the light of these facts that the team-teaching approach favoured by a majority of the teachers who took part in the research survey becomes so attractive. Using a variety of members of staff should ensure that a fairly wide diversity of first- and second-hand experience is available when moral education courses are being planned by a school. John Wilson offered the reminder that 'some of the most important factors which *produce* a morally educated person may have little to do with any direct process of moral education, or even with any *educational* process at all'.[4] Nevertheless, as he goes on to show, schools can make an important contribution to their pupils' moral development. At the end of his book, he and his colleagues list a number of practical suggestions for moral education lessons. These include courses about other people as well as helping children to analyse moral principles or the reasons for the choices made in certain given contexts. As he says, for instance, 'a course specifically designed (say) to teach children what other people feel, or to help them to make up moral rules in particular situations, would (if it worked at all) be directly beneficial.'[5]

L

Much will depend on the way a school is organised, and on the atmosphere it fosters, since these factors affect the pupils considerably. For the bonds and pressures of every school community are primarily moral. If discipline is poor, and discordant, unco-operative attitudes prevail, then both the academic work will suffer and the school's moral influence will be adverse. If positive standards are to be communicated, the life and tone of a school must likewise be good. This means that the schools will have to determine which moral principles they intend to advocate and to teach. They must also decide upon the kind of character traits they wish to commend to their pupils. As Professor P. H. Hirst points out, 'until we are clearer as to the level at which we have agreement, we have no satisfactory basis for moral education. We therefore need to formulate these principles, to sort out the concepts involved and the logic of moral reasoning ... We must also look again at the factual knowledge about society and personal relationships without which it is impossible for pupils to learn to make responsible moral judgments ... And we shall have to formulate programmes of work which can provide not only basic moral understanding but also some basic moral training. It is surely quite obvious that satisfactory education in this area is not a merely intellectual matter. A school community necessarily provides a moral training and we need to examine and quite deliberately replan what goes on, with positive aims in mind.'[6]

Research has shown that most teachers regard the moral education of children as extremely important, and a clear majority from all sections of the profession desire to give more positive help than is generally available at present in the schools. What then should be done next? Professor Hirst's remarks suggest some of the main answers to this question. Concerning content, St. Paul has a piece of advice relevant to all subjects on the curriculum of any school, but especially pertinent to the subject of moral education. He urged his Philippian readers: 'Whatever is true, whatever is honourable, whatever is just, whatever is pure, whatever is lovely, whatever is gracious, if there be any excellence, if there is anything worthy of praise, think about these things.'[7] Positive moral development is more likely to take place if our pupils concentrate on what is good rather than what is evil, sordid and corrupt. The latter soils, the former enlightens.

On the other hand, this does not mean that children should be protected completely from having to face up to difficult, even painful issues. A central part of moral development concerns the making of decisions some of which one may well want to avoid if possible. The moral education of pupils must include helping them to recognise and tackle these problems. How should the teachers introduce their pupils to painful situations? When should difficult issues be raised? How far should children be protected from or exposed to some of the harsher facts of life? There is no easy answer to any of these queries. It is surely right always to try to prevent them from coming into contact with the corrupt, or even anything which coarsens or degrades. But certain hard, unpleasant issues have to be acknowledged and discussed from time to time.

The need to respect the feelings and consciences of one's pupils is paramount in all the teaching that is done. The warnings which respondents to the survey gave about preaching must be kept clearly in mind. Obviously one does not present problems for discussion in ways which virtually rub the children's noses in them. Much care is required to prevent pupils from being needlessly shocked or worried. The best approach will always be sensitive and sympathetic. For just as the whole attitude of the teacher must be a caring one, so part of the teaching task in moral education lessons is to try to create compassionate attitudes in the children. Also the sense of wonder which most children retain during their school years can be fostered and shared. It can so easily be destroyed by unthinking or cynical comments and attitudes. Likewise the magic that is present in so many situations, relationships and areas of new knowledge. As the deputy head from a Bristol school reminded us in Chapter 9, we need to respect and protect the innocence of children.

Schools must also respect and beware of teaching against the wishes of the parents in all aspects of moral education. The danger of encroaching too much on the role and authority of the parent has to be borne in mind. So it will probably be advisable to consult parents about any proposals to have special time for moral education as part of the school curriculum. The educational value of much that is planned will be readily obvious to many parents. Explanations should be given to make clear to them exactly what is envisaged. It may even be necessary, as with religious knowledge lessons, to give them the opportunity to withdraw their pupils from some or all of these lessons should they wish to do so. For if these periods are to be of real help to the pupils, the co-operation of the parents is essential.

At which stages of a child's school life is he to have these direct moral education lessons? As was seen earlier in the book, most teachers favoured the period of secondary education as the best time, though some thought that primary school children would be helped also, as long as the content and methods of these lessons were appropriate to the needs and level of understanding of the pupils. Such a condition applies to these sessions whatever the age group involved. The fact that there are sex differences in attitudes and approaches to moral issues, would have to be reckoned with. Also much would depend on what was being taught. Our growing understanding of children's moral development appears to reinforce the case for more conscious moral education in school at *every* stage. The intelligent use of 'form periods' by teachers in many primary and secondary schools, in which moral problems and issues of personal relationships are sometimes raised, shows that time can be profitably spent on these matters at all levels. If special lessons were set aside for moral education, however these periods were titled,

156

the chance would then have been created for all children to benefit. More guidance would be necessary from those who study child development, along with more effective ways of communicating to teachers the latest research findings on such questions as how children learn.

One area of study, briefly hinted at earlier in the book and well worth the attention of every teacher, from the nursery school to the university, is that concerned with social interaction. Many psychologists rightly insist that all children need help in the formation of identity, especially during adolescence. The whole experience of school, not merely what is taught there, influences every child in the development of his or her concept of self. In all this, relationships with others are obviously vital, and should therefore be subjected to a closer scrutiny by teachers, an examination based, if possible, on the knowledge of current research findings in this field. Michael Argyle, for instance, is very helpful here.[8] He argues that social competence has a number of identifiable components in which training might be given. He cites the motivational, the perceptual, response patterns, and matters of self confidence and self-preservation. He suggests that it is possible not only to modify social anxiety in a person but also to give social skills which make successful dominance possible in a relationship. Rightly stressing that far too little educational effort is put into helping pupils to learn non-verbal skills, he recommends, at the perceptual level, training which aims to make pupils more aware of the non-verbal as well as the verbal elements of interaction. They might be taught strategies of assessing social situations and how to interpret cues correctly. In all this, children would need to be shown how to take the role of the other person during interaction, and to practise this role playing.

Patterns of response in social interaction should be analysed in particular to try to decide the reasons for the success or failure of different approaches. Children should also be helped to present themselves effectively to others, and to develop increased confidence in themselves. Positive teaching, backed by praise and other rewards, is likely to be more successful here than are negative methods. Of a number of approaches that Argyle lists, there are several relevant to the classroom, in addition to the usual educational methods such as lectures, discussions, reading, private study and instructional films and tapes. He mentions learning on the job, the most common way of mastering social skills, and points out that coaching and feedback are essential to general success here. Secondly he underlines the value of role-playing and simulation in which pupils, when they take these sessions seriously, may not only learn specific social skills, but can be trained to observe others in varying situations. A third suggestion involves what he calls 'other sensitivity training' which might involve such activities as analysing emotional tones of speech, the choice of verbal expressions, the use of the eyes to convey attitudes and information, and the cues that bodily posture can suggest. Argyle wonders whether behaviour may become more contrived and insincere when people are trained to interact better. He also asks whether people will be manipulated by those practising the new skills. Such results are indeed possible. Nevertheless he rightly concludes that many difficulties and frustrations in social interaction could be eliminated if people had a wider understanding of, and better training in, the skills involved in living and mixing with others.

To leave the moral education of pupils to indirect means is not enough, even though much can be done in various ways, as the teachers showed in Chapter 8. For it is not certain that much *will* be done, especially in schools where examination and specialisation pressures are strong. In such circumstances pupils can easily be starved of moral discussion. Science and geography are primarily concerned with what is, not what ought to be. Economics tells us how money works and how different trading systems operate, not who should have the money or whether we ought to tamper with the current system to make it better on moral grounds. Sociology describes various kinds of society for us, but is not competent to say what is the *best* society. Psychology studies behaviour patterns for us, but cannot tell us what sort of adults we ought to produce. Both these last two studies are being introduced in elementary forms into more and more school timetables now.

Even in subjects where moral issues are much more likely to be present, attention may well be focused elsewhere. History deals with real people and real situations, and some moral judgments must be passed. Yet there are so many facts to be learned, and syllabuses are so wide that there is no time really to consider the moral problems involved. Literature, with classics in school, was one traditional way in which the young absorbed moral values. Classics has now nearly disappeared from the school curriculum. Literature is studied today much more for its own sake and for amusement. The purpose that many writers and dramatists had, along with the tellers of myths, legends and old stories of the race – to introduce and examine aspects of the ethical inheritance of a nation – is often forgotten or ignored. In any case subjects like history, literature and religion seem to be given far less time on school timetables than other studies. Yet the central core of our ethical traditions is here.

Therefore it is very important that pupils should be given the chance in school to sit back and consider moral principles and their outworking in practice. Despite the rush to master all the knowledge and skills required to pass the various examinations, the personal should not be shut out. Other pressures will have to be restricted so that more time may be given to consider personal relationships. It is not enough to expect (as some do) the religious knowledge specialists to undertake this in their lessons. Most of them do, but the parsimonious allowance of time that is given to many of them means that they cannot cope adequately with all the relevant aspects of moral education as well. They have too little time to cover their own syllabuses to their satisfaction. As was said at the beginning of the book, teachers are concerned firstly to help make men and women. It follows that they must have time to study with their pupils what is good and true, pure and beautiful, what constitutes good character and maturity, and where possible the principles underlying these matters. Pupils also need to be made aware of the non-rational elements involved in moral decision-making. Given this time, one result might well be a more balanced education for most children.

So much for moral education. Lastly, what about the teachers? What great demands all this makes upon them! Because the moral education of children is so vital, the teaching must be of high quality. Whoever takes these lessons, therefore, will have to be well-equipped both as specialists and as individuals. They should be both skilled practitioners and persons of integrity. How right were those employers and school governors of old in laying the greatest stress on the character of the teachers rather than on their qualifications.[9] If special moral education lessons become part of school timetables, then more help must be given to teachers during their period of professional training, and in in-service courses. Student teachers tend to be more concerned to acquire technical skills than anything else. Yet their personal education is crucial also. Establishments of higher education need to remember that in their work with their students they should be as concerned about personality development as about academic excellence. More attention will have to be paid to the proper equipping of teachers to enable them to contribute to moral education courses. This may well mean more emphasis being laid upon certain relevant aspects of philosophy, psychology and sociology in training programmes. But there will have to be more stressing of *personal* development at all stages of their education. Too often this is taken for granted, especially in tertiary education.

For teaching children is a tremendous privilege. Teachers are more answerable than many in other occupations and professions. Even if they wanted to, they could not really opt out of the great responsibilities and privileges given to them. These demands and opportunities are most obviously seen in connection with the personal moral development of their pupils. For they highlight the fact that teaching is still a calling, demanding intelligence, enterprise, imagination, vision and hard work. With such qualities in the teachers, the influence of moral education upon the children in our maintained schools should be positive and beneficial, not only for the individual pupils, but also for the society in which they live. For as the Book of Proverbs also points out – in Chapter 14, verse 34 – it is righteousness that exalts a nation.

REFERENCES

1. E. M. and M. EPPEL, *Adolescents and Morality*, Routledge and Kegan Paul, 1966, p. 221.
2. L. BERKOWITZ, *The Development of Motives and Values in the Child*, Basic Books Inc., 1964, p. 57.
3. R. S. PETERS, *Ethics and Education*, Allen and Unwin, 1966, p. 173.
4. JOHN WILSON *et al.*, *Introduction to Moral Education*, Penguin Books, 1967, p. 139.
5. Ibid., pp. 448–449.
6. P. H. HIRST, 'The Curriculum', in *The Educational Implications of Social and Economic Change*, The Schools Council Working Paper No. 12, H.M.S.O., 1967, p. 79.
7. Philippians, Chapter 4, verse 8, R.S.V.
8. MICHAEL ARGYLE: *Social Interaction*, Methuen, 1969. See especially, Chapter X.
9. See, for example, FOSTER WATSON, *The English Grammar Schools to 1660*, C.U.P., 1908, pp. 127–131.

Chapter 14

Suggestions for Content and Methods

In this book, two main tasks have been attempted. The first was to examine the whole question of moral education in school and to consider the arguments for doing more to help children's moral development than is at present attempted in most primary and secondary schools. The second purpose of the book was to describe in some detail the views of teachers concerning moral education. It is fair to say that a strong case can be made out for more specific moral teaching in our schools. Such teaching, as the weight of research evidence shows, receives the support of many teachers throughout the country. A substantial majority clearly believes that something more definite needs to be done about the moral education of their pupils. As the report in Chapter 11 demonstrates, a considerable majority of 14- to 16-years-olds agrees with them. There is plenty of evidence that many teachers are still somewhat at sea in their own thinking about the subject. No matter how convincing they may believe arguments to be which champion the cause of moral education in school, what they really want to know in the end is precisely what to do in moral education lessons and how to do it.

It is hardly possible here to attempt to provide very detailed suggestions about content and methods, but certain proposals will be outlined. There is an urgent need for a number of moral education textbooks suitable for different age groups. However, some practical help will certainly be forthcoming in the next year or two from the Schools Council moral education curriculum development project. This research team has already devised much material which is being tested in schools, and which should soon be published. We can also expect further suggestions from the Farmington Trust researchers. Meanwhile there is nothing to prevent interested teachers, working individually and in groups, from attempting to devise material of their own, and trying it out in school as and when opportunities arise. They know the pupils for whom they would be creating such tasks, their needs, interests and current stage of development. Furthermore, as has been demonstrated in this book, many of them have plenty of ideas about what might be done. Nevertheless most teachers would still welcome both general guidance and specific suggestions on the subject.

There are two preliminary matters which demand the attention of probably every teacher. In the first place we need to be quite clear about the educational objectives at which our schools should be aiming in all that they do for all their pupils. What do we really hope to achieve year by year with the children and young people in our care, as they go through the school? Also, what do we hope that they will be like as persons when they finally say goodbye to us? When they leave, as well as having reached different levels of academic attainment, they will each have a value system of their own and attitudes to life, to work, to others and towards themselves. These will probably not be fully formed or necessarily consistent, and some of them will never be able to work out a fully coherent system of standards and values for themselves. Has the school contributed to the development of each of its pupils' value system? If so, in what ways? Such questions lead to the second matter which all teachers perhaps ought to think through. Since the moral education of children is going on all the time in school, exactly how does the school influence the moral development of its pupils? What exactly are the values which teachers wish to impress upon children? What effects, in so far as these can be assessed, do teaching, learning and the school community life have upon all concerned? Perhaps a fairer, or a somewhat easier question is: what effects do we want the learning, teaching and living together to have upon our pupils?

If we can arrive at reasonably lucid answers to such queries as these, then we shall be in a better position to assess the contribution that we hope specific moral education lessons will make in the upbringing of the nation's children, especially the ones in our care. For the clearer we are about the general educational objectives of school life and the part played by every aspect of each school day in achieving these goals, so we shall be more able to decide what it is we should like our pupils to learn in their moral education periods.

It is reasonable to look to psychologists for increasing help in understanding children's moral development, as more and more research is carried out on this aspect of children's growth. Such findings as have been achieved are neither precise nor sure enough to use as prescriptions of what to do. But they can sharpen our insight into the complex problem of children's moral development, and clarify our thinking on the subject. In the development of moral character, various important influences play their part. The impact of home guidance is vital, especially in the first years of life, in helping children, usually by means of rewards and punishment, to control their impulses. As the child's world expands, he learns much by identifying with and imitating others who impress him favourably and to whom he feels strong emotional attachment. The older he gets the stronger becomes the influence of peer and other social groups, who introduce him to a variety of moral values. If he is to reach moral maturity, however, he must be able to think rationally and analytically about moral issues. He should receive considerable help from the school in developing his powers of reflective thinking.

There are other important details which research has revealed. Moral behaviour is often the outcome of decisions determined by the factors of a particular situation. If the factors vary, so may the conduct, whatever the professed standards of the individual concerned. Attitude to self, ability to concentrate, self-control, ability to look ahead, to be patient and wait for better and greater gains rather than enjoying immediate and perhaps inferior satisfaction, all influence moral behaviour. Because pupils display morally conforming behaviour, it does not follow that such conduct is always the outcome of sound, mature moral beliefs which exercise control. External conditions will frequently influence a person's decision to conform or not to conform, as well as the internal standards he has. Intellectual development is an important factor in developing moral judgment, but a child's particular level of moral judgment is distinctive and is not just dependent either on his intellectual level or his home background.

Various writers have suggested criteria which, they claim, characterise the morally mature person. There is general agreement that perhaps the most obvious of these is the ability to consider the feelings and interests of others as well as one's own. A second criterion is the ability to grasp and if necessary to modify moral principles. Thirdly there is the ability to take account of the facts of any situation and to act with clear awareness of the likely consequences. John Wilson proposes a further criterion, the ability to be lucid and logical in the use of language. Consequently the morally mature person will be a rational, responsible, morally autonomous individual who acts with the welfare and interests of others clearly in mind.

These criteria provide goals towards which those who take moral education lessons can aim. With the guidance provided by psychological researchers, they also suggest ideas for both the content and methods relevant to such lessons. All this information further helps to correct any tendency to think that moral education is a subject in the same way that other parts of the school timetable can be so described. As was argued in chapter three, moral judgments form a logically self-contained area of discourse which is *sui generis*. There are a limited number of distinctive fields of knowledge one of which is the moral, and if children are to receive a fully-rounded education in school, we therefore need to assist their moral understanding and growth. Nevertheless, as John Wilson rightly points out, 'we have to rid ourselves of the temptation to think that there is a *thing called* "moral education" which exists over and above particular activities designed to elicit particular skills'.[1]

It is worth pointing out that moral education lessons should not be conceived of simply as a means towards inculcating self-discipline and good habits generally, aims which often characterise the work of Sunday schools, scout and guide movements and the like. Research findings, by Hartshorne and May[2] and others following them, have again and again shown that such moral training of the type often attempted in the past by youth organisations has little real effect upon children's moral conduct. Yet one should not infer from these results that such character education has no effective influence whatsoever upon moral development. What teachers of moral education can aim for is to help their pupils to develop their own moral judgment and to encourage them to determine their own conduct on the basis of internalised moral principles. This involves assisting pupils gradually to develop through the different stages of moral growth from one level of maturity to the next, and to learn to assess their own and other people's behaviour on a foundation of developing moral judgment.

166

What, then, can teachers profitably do in moral education lessons? As was noted in Chapter 2, many of the suggestions made by teachers showed that the word 'moral' was interpreted in four main ways – philosophical, social, religious and sexual. These classifications are not very helpful when one attempts to analyse the content of moral education. Sexual morality is only a very limited part of the social aspect. There is undoubtedly an intimate connection between religion and morality, but it might be better to discuss the religious aspects of moral judgment and conduct in concurrent religious education periods. From the classroom point of view it may be more useful to consider possible material and activities under three main headings, philosophical training, personal training and social training. Let us now briefly examine each of these in turn. It is worth adding that these headings serve merely as approximate guides. Some material proposed under one heading could well also find a place under another.

Under the heading 'philosophical training' something can be included for younger and less able children as well as for older and academically gifted pupils. All children need to consider the question of rules of conduct, to appreciate how necessary and helpful they are for young and old alike, to come to see that some are expedient and temporary while others have permanent relevance, and to discover for themselves if possible the fact that obedience leads to freedom. They might discuss rules for the classroom, the laboratory, the playground and the highway, for the school community, for work in different kinds of employment (including something on contracts between employers and employees), for games and for society as a whole, not forgetting international rules. Information might be given about the law of the land, especially as it affects the lives of the young, and different ethical codes might be studied. There could also be some discussion about the nature and purpose of punishment, and the value of rewards. Pupils should be introduced gradually to moral concepts and language. Older ones should be helped to define terms and to analyse the different ways in which people use them. With these pupils, ethical principles can be examined along with questions of authority, freedom, responsibility, duty and obligation, and specific moral qualities. Younger children also can learn to consider particular virtues, such as honesty, kindness, respect for others, etc., especially if these are presented in the form of concrete examples rather than abstract theories. Such teaching could be linked with the study of different standards and values, some analysis of which will in any case be undertaken in other subject lessons. Finally, again in the secondary school, pupils might be trained to examine all the different external conditions which influence behaviour as they study varying situations and problems. By means of practical illustrations they can learn to support judgments with proper evidence, and come to understand something of the complexity of much decision-making.

Most teachers would argue that the personal training of pupils goes on all the time in school. Can anything specifically directed to moral development be done in moral education periods? As several writers on problems of moral education have pointed out, balanced moral judgments are not made in a vacuum. They require a firm basis in fact. Part of the task of helping children to progress in moral understanding, therefore, must be to assist them to acquire clear factual information, especially about themselves and their environment. Work suitable to the age and understanding of each class could be done about the human body – human physiology and sex education lessons – to supplement (if necessary) study already undertaken in science lessons. Then, as some teachers in the research survey suggested, older pupils might be introduced to some elementary psychology concerning the ways in which individuals develop intellectually, emotionally and morally, and how attitudes are formed and changed. Much needs to be attempted with all pupils in educating the emotions, training in judgment and practice in the exercise of responsibility and self-control. The development of feeling, of character, of the concept of self, entails a lot of work with individual pupils, since sharp individual differences are usually present in all classes, even when children are of similar ability and come from similar backgrounds. Pupils can study particular emotions and the way they can affect behaviour both by examining examples from literature and drama and by considering invented illustrations based on situations that children typically experience. Linked with this last point would be opportunities to analyse the different ways it would be possible to act in certain familiar situations. The aim in all this would be to deepen awareness of human personality and encourage greater understanding of the human condition. Pupils would also come to appreciate the notion of responsible choice, learning to consider which choices in different situations are significant.

The overlap at these points between personal and social training is obvious. The two go together for much of the time. Social training would be specially concerned with helping children to understand and at appropriate points to identify with others. The time might be spent in some lessons by examining the rights and duties of different individuals and groups, at home, at school, at work, at play. Varied examples of social conduct and manners could be considered, using case studies of individuals, biographies and illustrations from family, group and mass behaviour. Different situations might be described in which the value of consistent, considerate action can be demonstrated. Much practical work could be done on the problems of assessment of others, using illustrations from the work of teachers, employers, youth leaders and magistrates. Questions about friendships and marriage, about relationships – between children and adults, pupils and teachers, employers and employees, neighbours, etc. – and about the problems facing minority groups in society might be discussed and explored. Also different conceptions of what is a 'good' person. Matters of social planning and organisation at local authority and national levels might be scrutinised with their many personal and ethical considerations, such as the moral issues underlying techno-logical decisions or the conflict which can arise between per-sonal interests and those of society in the building of new motorways, new towns and town centres, new factories, etc. Leisure-time activities and the mass media provide still more material which can suitably be discussed in moral education lessons.

It should not be too difficult to plan, especially for older pupils, a year's programme of lessons for different age-groups on the basis of these suggestions for content. But before glanc-ing at possible methods of teaching this material, it is worth asking what are the particular abilities and skills which such a course of moral education lessons would hope to foster. Earlier in the chapter reference was made to what certain people have said are the four main criteria of the morally mature individual. Is it possible to decide in greater detail what attainments we wish pupils to achieve through moral education? Norman Williams has offered valuable suggestions about the component factors involved in moral behaviour,[3] and they are included in the list below. Then, as a basis for discussion and for classroom experiment, a framework has been devised in tabular form in which the activities for moral education lessons and the skills they are intended to develop, have been grouped under their three headings. Beside each activity a possible age-range has been suggested for which that activity might be suitable. The whole scheme is very tentative. The groupings are not mutually exclusive and there is much more overlapping than is indicated. Yet if it provides a starting point for action, or a stimulus to seek a more refined plan, it will have served a useful purpose.

170

Abilities to be fostered in Moral Education Lessons

The ability:	to form and use moral concepts.
(Philosophical)	to reason morally, to make rational judgments.
	to develop moral principles, relating to one's own and other people's interests.
(Personal)	to develop ego-controls, and mastery of self.
	to understand self – physical and emotional development, and to develop the concept of self.
	to master relevant factual knowledge, and learn to amass and use evidence.
(Social)	to relate emotionally to others – identify and sympathise with others.
	to learn from experience – one's own and other people's.
	to make rational assessment – of others and of 'moral' situations.
	to predict consequences.

All leading to the ability to act in a reasonable, independent, morally mature way.

TABLE 16

Type of training	Suggested age-range	Activities	Skills
Philo-sophical training.	9–12	Examining and making up rules, laws, etc.	Ability to form concepts, to reason morally. Develop moral principles.
	9–14	Study of moral virtues – honesty, kindness, etc., and some vices – selfishness, telling lies, etc.	Develop moral principles, learn to make rational judgments.
	10–16	Study conditions influencing behaviour.	Ability to amass and use evidence, and make rational assessments.
	13–16	Definition of terms.	Concept formation and use.
	13–16	Discussion sessions – on concepts, ideas of authority, responsibility, freedom, etc.	Concept formation. Making rational judgments. Develop moral principles.
Personal training.	7–14	Role-playing.	Understanding of self and others. Mastery of self.
	9–16	Fact-learning about environment.	Understanding of self. Ability to predict consequences.
	10–12	Fact-learning about human body and reproduction.	Ability to develop ego-controls, self-concept. Mastery of self.
	13–16	Learning about human development.	Understanding of self and others. Develop self-concept, self-mastery.
	13–16	Study of emotions.	Develop self-concept. Understanding human nature.

Type of training	Suggested age-range	Activities	Skills
Social training.	7–14	Role-playing.	Ability to assess and identify with others.
	8–14	Story-completion tasks, etc.	To make rational assessments, develop moral judgments, predict consequences.
	8–16	Helping others, assuming responsibility.	Ability to learn from experience. Identify with others, make rational assessments.
	8–16	Visits, talks.	Master relevant factual knowledge, learn from others' experience.
	9–16	Examining case-studies, biographies, character sketches.	Ability to relate emotionally, make rational assessments, learn from others' experience.
	9–16	Studying relationships of all kinds, minority group problems, etc.	Ability to understand and identify with others, and to predict consequences.
	13–16	Debating. Arguing for particular viewpoints.	Ability to identify with others, make rational judgments, use evidence.

Much of this work is concerned with the development of attitudes and values. Children begin to learn these from their earliest years. Most attitudes are closely concerned with particular preferences and longings, but moral attitudes are more specifically related to absolute obligations of 'must' and 'ought' and 'should'. How far teachers in moral education lessons should aim deliberately to change pupil attitudes is a controversial issue. What they surely can try to do is to help their pupils to recognise and understand different points of view and to realise some of the consequences which might follow from acting in accordance with these viewpoints. In other words, as was suggested above, they would be assisting children and young people to develop to positions in which they are equipped to make responsible choices.

To aim so far but no farther is probably to avoid the possible charge of indoctrination. The old, authoritarian methods referred to in Chapter 2 and used by some in the past are obviously unsuitable. Such approaches do not educate. The arbitrary demand that children accept and conform to a set of individual or social standards imposed upon them from without will do nothing to encourage true moral development. The question 'How does one teach moral education?' becomes easier to answer when one has a clearer idea of the possible content of moral education lessons. Indeed it is really not a proper question at all. One does not teach moral education. One teaches a variety of topics and encourages pupils to engage in a variety of activities which should contribute to their moral development. M. G. Hinton has argued that 'as a teaching technique, the pragmatic approach to questions of morals is almost always to be preferred to the deductive'.[4] This is especially true for younger pupils. Just as with spiritual, mental and physical education, so in moral education teachers must take account of the stage of development which their pupils have reached. They must teach material and set tasks which are suitable to that stage, whether it be the prudential, the authoritarian, the reciprocal (in which children begin to act with consideration for others) or the social. This will mean that in some lessons different pupils will be doing different work, involving either individual or group teaching or both.

It is quite likely that in personal training pupils will learn more by the actual experience of helping others and assuming responsibility, and by the imaginative acting out of different roles, than by analytic study of moral situations. Nevertheless in philosophical and social training a variety of approaches may be adopted with profit. There will be sessions of straightforward information giving and finding. There will also be much discussion, especially with older pupils, of current social problems and moral situations. Other kinds of oral work can help children to experience the feelings and points of view of others. The dramatisation of set and spontaneously invented situations is particularly useful here. In this way pupils can experience something of the problems and attitudes of other people – those who represent authority, for instance, or who wish to state a particular case. Debates, mock interviews and mock trials are valuable aids. Different individual and group exercises can be devised – exploring typical situations familiar to children and young people to discover variant ways of behaviour or to arrive at definite moral judgments. Story completion tasks and other published test material used by researchers in character development may often provide helpful exercises. It is fairly easy to obtain such material from libraries. There will be periods for reading biographical and other literary extracts which illustrate aspects of character or which depict emotion or relationships. In such lessons the English teacher's question: Is this authentically described? will be as relevant as moral questions like: Is that a fair, right, considerate action or attitude? Inventing rules for specific groups or situations and making up new games are useful exercises for older primary and younger secondary school children. Then, especially if the moral education lessons are timetabled at the end of a morning or afternoon, visits can be arranged to gain factual knowledge of a locality and its problems, or to study the ways in which different groups in society are cared for. Also, films depicting different problems which face children can be shown and talks about their work may be given by outside speakers such as clergy, police, magistrates, doctors, local administrators and social workers.

Some of these suggestions have been made by others, and many of them link up easily with work being done by teachers in other lessons. There are very close connections with the content of many religious knowledge, literature, history, science and social studies periods. This fact reinforces the majority view of teachers taking part in the research survey that team-teaching is a good way to organise moral education lessons. It also serves as an extra reminder that such special periods in no way replace the indirect moral training taking place in the

174

school. A further fact is worth stressing concerning methods of teaching. Just as it is important that children should have read a good deal of poetry of various kinds before we ask them to write much verse of their own, so the ground must be prepared, usually through experience, before children may be expected to analyse and discuss moral questions. They need such a basis to make discussion more meaningful and as a springboard for future progress.

It may well be many years before moral education lessons become an accepted part of school timetables, despite the strong case that can be made out for such periods. As the research survey described in this book has demonstrated, many doubts still have to be conquered. Even where sympathy for the proposal is shown, help and guidance are necessary. This means that all teacher training programmes should include courses on children's moral development. In addition, student teachers should be given detailed assistance concerning material and methods which will promote their pupils' moral growth. In-service courses on moral education should also be provided for practising teachers at both primary and secondary levels. More research needs to be done on the whole problem. The work of the Farmington Trust and Schools Council teams should be extremely valuable in producing immediate help and in tracing lines of future development.

The role of the teacher in our schools today has become exceedingly complex. The cautionary advice that James gives in the third chapter of his New Testament letter is pertinent indeed. He says: 'Let not many of you become teachers, my brethren, for you know that we who teach shall be judged with greater strictness. For we all make many mistakes. . . .'[5] Many may feel that his counsel applies particularly to teachers of moral education. His words underline the high qualities of character and ability which the office of teacher demands, whatever one's subject may be. For no schoolmaster or mistress is

175

merely the teacher of a subject. All contribute to the general upbringing of all their pupils, and in particular to their moral development. Education is most of all a matter of personal relationships. To attempt more specific help in children's moral understanding and judgment is to re-emphasise the significance of this fact. But moral education also stresses standards of what is good and right and true. With all the other work being done in school it can play a part in providing vision in education. For with what is moral education most concerned? It is with personal character and judgment, social relationships, obligations and vision. And is not that, in the end, also what life is all about?

REFERENCES

1. JOHN WILSON, *Introduction to Moral Education*, Penguin Books, 1967, p. 140.

2. H. HARTSHORNE and M. A. MAY, *Studies in the Nature of Character*, 3 vols., Macmillan (New York), 1928–30.

3. *Introduction to Moral Education*, Penguin Books, 1967, pp. 287–289.

4. M. G. HINTON, 'Religious Education and the Teaching of Morality', in *Moral Education in Schools*, published for the General Studies Association by Longmans, 1968, pp. 24–35. See p. 32.

5. Epistle of James, Chapter 3, verses 1 and 2. R.S.V.

Appendix A

Below are listed all the main questions on moral education that were asked in the questionnaires sent out in the research survey among teachers. The answers to these questions are discussed in the main body of the book, especially Chapters 4, 6, 7 and 8.

MORAL EDUCATION IN SCHOOL

24. Indirect moral education in school comes via (Please *number* in order of importance those of the following suggestions you agree with):

Literature lessons	☐
The study of history	☐
Music and Art lessons	☐
Social studies/civics	☐
The individual teacher whatever his subject	☐
Games and sports	☐
Positions of responsibility	☐

Any other suggestions? (Not to be numbered)

25. Special periods (not including religious knowledge periods) should be set aside in state schools for moral education. (Please tick the suggestion(s) you agree with)

for all junior school year groups (7+ to 11+)	☐
for the 10+ to 11+ year group only, in junior schools	☐
only in secondary schools	☐
for all secondary school year groups	☐
for 13+ to 16+ year groups	☐
for VI form groups	☐
not at all	☐

26. If special periods are set aside in state schools for moral education, they should be taken only by members of staff who are willing to do so

Strongly Agree ☐
Agree ☐
Uncertain ☐
Disagree ☐
Strongly Disagree ☐

27. Special periods for moral education should be taken in state schools by (Please tick the suggestion(s) you agree with)

the head teacher ☐
the religious knowledge teacher(s) ☐
the class/form teachers ☐
all members of staff ☐
several members of staff working as a team ☐
No one ☐

28. If special periods are set aside in state schools for moral education they should be unconnected with religious instruction periods

Strongly Agree ☐
Agree ☐
Uncertain ☐
Disagree ☐
Strongly Disagree ☐

29. The content of moral education in state schools should include: (*number* in order of importance those of the following suggestions you agree with)

teaching about general ethical principles ☐
teaching about the law of the land ☐
teaching about Christian ethics ☐
teaching about sexual morality ☐
discussion of relations between children and adults ☐
discussion of case studies ☐

Any other suggestions? (Not to be numbered)

30. Many organisations provide opportunities for social service for children and young people. State schools should also provide opportunities for social service for their pupils.

Strongly Agree ☐
Agree ☐
Uncertain ☐
Disagree ☐
Strongly Disagree ☐

31. If state schools provide opportunities for social service for their pupils, pupils should take part:

– only on a voluntary basis ☐
– as and when expected to do so ☐

32. If you think that specific moral education lessons should *not* be given in state schools, please state the reason(s) which you feel most strongly support(s) this opinion

Appendix B

Here are the questions on moral education in school that were posed to the random sample of 14- to 16-year-old pupils in maintained schools throughout England. Analysis and discussion of the answers to these questions can be found in Chapter 11.

(1) People have suggested many things that they think the schools should do to help young people. Here are some of their suggestions. Please say what you think about *each one* of them by putting a tick (√) in the column which fits your opinion.

Suggestion	Strongly Agree	Agree	Don't Know	Disagree	Strongly Disagree
1. Help you to do as well as possible in exams.	( )	( )	( )	( )	( )
2. Teach things to help you get a good job or career.	( )	( )	( )	( )	( )
3. Teach you about different sorts of jobs to help you to decide what to do when you leave school.	( )	( )	( )	( )	( )
4. Help you to develop your character and personality.	( )	( )	( )	( )	( )
5. Teach you about what is right and wrong.	( )	( )	( )	( )	( )
6. Teach you how to behave and make you feel at ease with others.	( )	( )	( )	( )	( )

Moral Education in School

Suggestion	Strongly Agree	Agree	Don't Know	Disagree	Strongly Disagree
7. Help you to develop your intelligence.	( )	( )	( )	( )	( )
8. Help you to stand on your own feet and to rely on yourself.	( )	( )	( )	( )	( )
9. Help you to widen your interests.	( )	( )	( )	( )	( )
10. Teach things of direct use to you in your future job.	( )	( )	( )	( )	( )

Which of these ten suggestions would you choose as the *three* most important tasks of the school? Please ring the *three* appropriate numbers.

1 2 3 4 5 6 7 8 9 10

(2) If you could choose how to spend 2 to 3 periods of your timetable each week, which *one* of the following suggestions would you choose. (Put a tick (√) in the appropriate box.)

1. Have more work on your favourite subject.	( )
2. Have more work on your weakest subject.	( )
3. Have talks and discussions on matters of daily life which interest you (e.g. how to behave, relations with others, what is right and wrong, etc.)	( )
4. Have talks and discussions about careers.	( )
5. Have free periods for private study or reading.	( )
6. None of these suggestions.	( )

(3) Here is a list of subjects which could be considered in school in talks and discussions. Please say about *each one* whether *you* think it should be discussed in school or not, by putting a tick (√) under the heading which best fits your opinion.

	Should definitely be discussed	Might well be discussed	Should not be discussed at all
1. Friendship	( )	( )	( )
2. How people should behave	( )	( )	( )
3. The law of the land	( )	( )	( )
4. Christian teaching about behaviour	( )	( )	( )
5. Sex and marriage	( )	( )	( )
6. Relations between people (e.g. between young people and adults, employers and employees, neighbours, etc.)	( ) ( )	( ) ( )	( ) ( )
7. Family life	( )	( )	( )
8. Standards of right and wrong	( )	( )	( )
9. Rewards and punishments	( )	( )	( )
10. Authority and how to exercise it	( )	( )	( )
11. The qualities of a good person	( )	( )	( )
12. The use of leisure time	( )	( )	( )

What other subjects like these (if any) do you think ought to be discussed in school?

(6) Special periods (not including religious knowledge periods) should be set aside in school for moral education. Tick (√) the box which agrees with your opinion. (Moral education is concerned with learning about the way people behave, what people are like as persons, relationships between people, teaching about right and wrong, and so on.)

Strongly Agree ( ) Agree ( ) Don't Know ( ) Disagree ( ) Strongly Disagree ( )

Please state your main reason(s) why you think as you do.

(7) If special periods are set aside in school for moral education, they should be taken by: (Tick (√) the suggestion(s) you agree with)

1. The head teacher	( )
2. The religious knowledge teacher(s)	( )
3. The class/form teachers	( )
4. All members of staff	( )
5. Several members of staff working as a team	( )
6. A special member of staff who does not take you for other lessons	( )
7. Someone not on the staff of your school	( )

(8) Do you, in school, have talks and discussions on matters of daily life which interest you (e.g. how to behave in different situations, relations with others, what is right and wrong etc.)?

Ring the appropriate answer   Yes   No

If your answer is 'yes', when do you have these talks and discussions? Tick (√) the appropriate box or boxes)

1. In religious knowledge lessons	( )
2. In English lessons	( )
3. In lessons specially set aside for these	( )
4. In general studies lessons	( )
5. In civics or social studies lessons	( )

Any other times?

Do you have these talks and discussions: (Ring the appropriate answer)

Once or more per week   Occasionally   Very rarely

Index

APR